Dear Danny

Happy Cooking!

Catherine

Kitchen
CONFIDENCE

BY CATHERINE SLOMAN
(AKA BATTENBURGBELLE)

Matador
9 Priory Business Park,
Wistow Road, Kibworth Beauchamp,
Leicestershire. LE8 0RX
Tel: 0116 279 2299
Email: books@troubador.co.uk
Web: www.troubador.co.uk/matador
Twitter: @matadorbooks

ISBN 978 1838592 271

British Library Cataloguing in Publication Data.
A catalogue record for this book is available from the British Library.

Printed and bound in the UK by TJ International, Padstow, Cornwall
Cover design, book design, and layout by Gregory Swenson of Recipes4Rebels.com
Illustrations by Harry Stone of harrystoneillustrations.co.uk

Matador is an imprint of Troubador Publishing Ltd

This book is dedicated to my beloved daughter, Jessie, who inspired me to put down my wooden spoon and get writing.

Thank You, Thank You, Thank You

So many people have helped me get from a half-baked idea to an actual book. I am supremely grateful to Jessie for asking me to do it in the first place and for gently reminding me on a regular basis to get on with it. She's also offered great advice and an excellent proof-reading service. Thank you to David for waiting to eat his dinner until I had finished photographing everything and for his famous light hand on the tiller throughout this trip. Thank you to Greg Swenson for the wonderful design of this book, his patience in waiting for me to get my act together, all the amazing effort he put into bringing it to life, and his generosity and wisdom in helping me turn this into a book I am proud of. And to Harry Stone for his beautiful illustrations.

Thank you to my wonderful friend Jenny for contributing recipes, encouraging me every step of the way, and generally being my kitchen co-conspirator. Thanks also to my friends Roger Pizey and Christian Honor for inspiring me with their fabulous books and contributing a couple of recipes. And to those established chefs who have come to feel like friends, some of whose recipes I have included, and all of whose books I pore over on a regular basis: Richard Bertinet, Felicity Cloake, Sophie Grigson, Simon Hopkinson, Nigella Lawson, Jamie Oliver, Yotam Ottolenghi, Kenny Shopsin, and Nigel Slater.

Thank you to Cindy Etsell for helping me stop procrastinating and getting this over the line. And to my lovely friends who read early copies and gave me their invaluable thoughts - Alizay Gaffar, Andrew French, Catherine Pellegrino, Emma Verebelyi, Fran Lea, Jan Goodman and Jenny Hammerton. Thanks also to Ros Hodgkiss, grammar guru.

Contents

A Kitchen Love Affair

Maybe you rarely venture into the kitchen and enjoy just a passing acquaintance with your oven. Perhaps you're plain bored with your repertoire and see cooking as a chore rather than a passport to eternal joy and happiness. Or, heavens to Betsy, you might be bursting with culinary ambition, itching to reach the next level, and looking for a little help to get there. If one of these sounds like you, then this book is my take on ways you can get started, get better, and just maybe, get hooked.

It's all about building up your confidence in the kitchen. Much as I would love to create a world full of fellow food obsessives, this book is more about encouraging people just to give cooking a whirl. This whole project was inspired by my lovely daughter Jessie, who asked me to write up some recipes to take with her when she heads out into the world for university and beyond. It gradually evolved into an actual book as I started telling my friends about it (anyone who would listen really) and everyone told me to go for it.

The pressure was on....

So this is my personal selection of recipes, based around what we eat at home and the dishes that I keep coming back to time after time because they are sooooo great. I hope you'll find ideas that tickle your tastebuds and inspire you to turn that occasional date with the oven into a full blown love affair with your kitchen.

Happy cooking!

Obsessions and Confessions

I am passionate about food. Nothing floats my boat like pottering around the kitchen, experimenting with new ideas, and trying them out on any innocent bystander in the vicinity. I get a huge kick out of inspiring others to learn to love being in their kitchens, or at the very least to see cooking as so much more than an unwelcome entry on the daily to-do list of life. And at best, to see home cooking as a worthy and enjoyable alternative to the far-too-easy to reach takeaway menus in the kitchen drawer.

I'm always happy to rustle up a meal for the family and I love entertaining friends. Any excuse will do. It's a chance to try out new recipes, get people together around the kitchen table, have lots of fun and, ideally, chat endlessly about food, cooking, and recipes. They do it all around the world you know, regardless of race, colour, religion, or indeed any protected characteristics you can think of. I love it!

I teach bakery at the fantastic Bread Ahead Bakery School in London, I am a Bread Angel (we are a group of bakers running their own home baking businesses), I give Kitchen Confidence cookery classes, deliver baked goods locally, run a pop-up supper club, and do private catering. To blow my own trumpet for a moment - I have won prizes for my baking. There are several rather lovely trophies in my kitchen. When I'm not experimenting in my own kitchen, any chance to learn from the experts - progressing from basic skills to more advanced stuff like knife skills, baking bread and cakes, patisserie, pastry, cheese making (yes, really), oh, and a memorable day as a beer maker.

A confession: I didn't love food as a child.

My family would tell you that, on the rare occasions we ate out when I was a kid, we absolutely had to go somewhere that served fish and chips. And all hell would break loose if they presumed to put tartare sauce on the plate. At home, I would sneak the many bits of food I didn't like the look of to my brothers. I had to start cooking for myself when I left home and began to dabble a little and try different foods (discovering the "all you can eat for £5" on Sunday evening at the fantastic curry houses when I was a student in Manchester was a turning point).

It was only later that I started to really enjoy experimenting in the kitchen, obsessively tearing recipes out of newspapers and magazines and stockpiling cookbooks.

As Battenburgbelle, I've been writing a food blog for a few years, all about my adventures as a home cook - you'll find more recipes at battenburgbelle.com. And I do bake a rather good Battenburg cake. If you want to know more about what I'm up to these days, check out my Kitchen Confidence website www.kitchenconfidence.co.uk.

For your notes...

A Few Culinary Tips and Techniques

TIPS

Read the recipe!! I still occasionally get to a crucial point in my cooking, only to realise that I need one more lemon or a pinch of the one spice that's just run out. So I should take my own advice and you should too - always read your recipe all the way through before you get started. Make sure you have all the utensils you're going to need before you get started as well.

It's also worth checking whether you can get some of your preparation done ahead of time - this can be really handy, especially if you have guests coming and you don't want them fainting with hunger while you are stuck in the kitchen.

The recipes in this book serve four people unless I have said otherwise (although be aware, I am used to catering for a teenage girl with a modest appetite). And with pancakes you can make enough for 10 and find that two of you have wolfed the lot...

I've given approximate timings for the recipes - as you get more confident, you'll probably speed up on some of the techniques, so these are just a guide. The timer on your phone is your friend - it's easy to get distracted, especially if you're multi-tasking. All oven temperatures are for a fan oven. If you don't have a fan oven, increase the temperature by 20°C.

There isn't a separate vegetarian chapter, but there are plenty of meat-free recipes in the book and I've suggested alternative ways to make some of the meat-based recipes. There are both meat and fish recipes in the pasta and rice section too. That's just the way it turned out. Oh, and some of the pasta and rice dishes are main courses.

I've put useful tips and techniques with some of the recipes and please feel free to make notes - it's definitely ok to write in cookbooks.

If you're baking, it's important to preheat the oven and to weigh your ingredients accurately. For other recipes like baked chicken, fish pie, or risotto, you can change the quantities a bit. You'll get to know what works! There are a few rice-based recipes here - if you are saving some for the next day, it's really important to cool it down quickly (within an hour), get it in the fridge and then re-heat it until it's piping hot. You don't want food poisoning, believe me.

TECHNIQUES

Here are some of the key abbreviations and techniques you'll find in this book:

g = gram

ml = millilitre (weigh liquid, it's more reliable than using a measuring jug, e.g. 100ml weighs 100g)

tbsp = tablespoon or around 15g and, unless you're baking, guesswork will be fine

tsp = teaspoon or around 5g - again, approximately will do, except for baking

Knives: you don't need to buy expensive knives, but life is a lot easier in the kitchen if they are sharp. I have a steel for this, but you can use something like the rough bit of the base of a mug or a nail file.

Chopping boards: it's really important to use a clean chopping board, particularly if you're cooking meat and vegetables. If you have had raw meat on a chopping board, you must clean it thoroughly or use a different board before you start preparing your vegetables.

Roughly chopped: using a sharp knife, cut into more or less bite-sized pieces. When you're chopping any vegetables, it's easiest to give yourself a flat surface - so for example, if you're chopping an onion, cut it in half first, from the root to the top, remove the skin, then lay the onion halves flat on your chopping board.

Diced: a little smaller than roughly chopped.

Finely chopped: smaller again.

Slicing an onion: once you've cut the onion in half, place the pieces flat side down on your board and slice the onion into semicircles.

Deseeding a chilli: the easiest way to get the seeds out is cut the ends off the chilli, cut the chilli in half lengthways then run a teaspoon down the middle of the chilli to remove the seeds and any white pith.

Boiling: if your water (or other liquid) needs to be boiling (for example for cooking pasta or reducing the liquid in a sauce), the surface should be bubbling vigorously.

Simmering: much more gentle than boiling - you should just see some smaller bubbles on the surface of the liquid.

Salt: you shouldn't have too much salt in your diet. The NHS suggests around one teaspoon a day for an adult. I don't add salt when I cook vegetables and I've given guidance in the recipes for where I would add salt. I do add a little when I'm

cooking rice or pasta - about half a teaspoon for a recipe serving four people. Lots of the recipes say "season to taste" - you'll get to know what you like, as you experiment with different dishes.

Butter: unless I've specified unsalted butter (usually for baking), then either salted or unsalted will be fine.

Squeezing a lemon or lime: if you don't have a juicer, cut your lemon/lime in half and squeeze using your bare hands.

Separating eggs: you need two small bowls or cups for this. Tap the egg gently on the worktop to crack open the shell. Open the shell over the first bowl and keep the yolk in one half of the shell. Then let the white drip into the other bowl, transfer the yolk into the other half of the shell, again letting the white drip into the bowl. Repeat until all the white is in the bowl, then tip the yolk into the second bowl. Sounds more complicated than it is when you actually do it.

Whisking eggs: your whisk and bowl must be clean and completely dry, or your eggs just won't whisk up. Recipes call for different stages of egg whisking. If you need soft peaks, when you remove the whisk a peak will form then droop. For stiff peaks, the peak will stay pointing upwards.

Rubbing in: some recipes call for butter to be rubbed into flour. Cut the butter into small pieces (usually straight from the fridge, unless the recipe says otherwise). Add to the flour and use just your fingertips to gently rub the mixture together, lifting your mixture a little to add air. The mixture should look like breadcrumbs.

Folding: this is a baking method for combining a light ingredient with a heavier one while retaining as much air as possible. Use a metal spoon or rubber spatula to work gently in a figure of eight movement to combine your ingredients.

Lining a cake tin: if the tin needs to be greased, use a butter wrapper or a little butter on a small piece of foil or baking parchment and rub the butter all around the tin. If a round tin needs to be lined, place the tin on baking parchment, draw a line all around it, and then cut it out. If you are lining a loaf tin, cut a rectangle larger than your tin, place in the tin, and press into the corners. You'll have to do a bit of folding to line the tin neatly. If you get a taste for baking, you may want to invest in some ready made cake tin paper liners.

Cooling rack: when you start baking cakes, it's useful to have a cooling rack. It allows air to circulate under a cake or loaf of bread, preventing the dreaded soggy bottom. It also helps crisp up cookies. If you don't have one, you can use the tray from a grill pan or an oven shelf.

If in doubt on deciding which way to do something, I often Google "Felicity Cloake's perfect…" Felicity is a great food writer and she does lots of research on different methods so we don't have to.

In my opinion, there are no stupid questions - if there's something I haven't covered in this book, Google will almost certainly have the answer. If you're still not sure about a particular technique, where to get an ingredient or possible substitutes, there are loads of helpful articles and videos online. Google may even direct you to my website - you can contact me via the website (www.kitchenconfidence.co.uk).

For your notes...

A Healthy You, A Healthy Planet

A HEALTHY YOU

This section is about taking care of yourself and the world around you. I don't claim to be a nutritional expert - but there's some basic information below about eating a healthy, balanced diet. If you want to know more, the NHS Eat Well Guidance is really helpful (www.nhs.uk).

The NHS suggests you do the following:

* Eat at least five portions of fruit and vegetables a day
* Base your meals on starchy food like potatoes, bread, rice and pasta
* Include some dairy or dairy alternatives in your diet
* Eat some protein, such as beans, pulses, fish, eggs and meat
* Use unsaturated oils and spread, in moderation
* Sugar and salt should also be consumed in moderation
* Drink plenty of fluids, especially water (booze doesn't count)

A HEALTHY PLANET

Eating nutritiously goes hand in hand with eating sustainably. I can't promise that I get this right all the time, but I do my best and these tips are a great way to start reducing the impact of what you eat on the environment, save money, and make sure you eat healthily.

Cook your own food: you've taken the first step just by picking up this book. Learning to cook can really make a difference - you'll reduce the amount of convenience and processed food you consume. This book includes recipes for basics such as granola, salad dressing, pasta sauces and lots of other dishes you can easily make at home rather than buying them.

Eat locally and seasonally: buying your ingredients locally and when they're in season is cheaper, reduces the distance your food has to travel, and supports your local economy. It also means you'll eat tastier food, because you're more likely to be eating what's fresh at the right time of year. If you want to use an ingredient that's not in season, keep the environmental impact (and the price) down by choosing tinned, dried, or frozen goods rather than buying something that has travelled half way around the world.

Grow your own ingredients: even if you just grow some herbs in a pot in your kitchen, you will be reducing your impact on the environment. No food miles, no packaging. And there is something very satisfying about watching something you planted yourself, growing into something you can eat.

Buy organic, free-range and free trade when you can: there's a reason why some foods are cheap, but there's an always impact on your health and the environment, so when you can, choose to shop organic, free-range or fair trade. Try to avoid processed foods and cook from scratch as often as possible.

Reduce meat and fish consumption: research consistently shows that animal-based foods have a much greater impact on the environment than plant foods. This is not the place to go into detail about this (and I do eat some meat and fish, although I do try not to overdo it) - but in a nutshell (and yes, eating nuts is good for us), consuming less meat will help reduce deforestation, methane emissions from cows, greenhouse gas from fertiliser use, and cruelty to animals.

Food packaging: try to keep this to a minimum. Supermarkets are getting better, but you can choose to buy food that's not over-packaged. Buying from local greengrocers, independent shops and markets also tends to keep the packaging down. They generally pay farmers more too.

Keep food waste to a minimum: you can really make a difference here - there are suggestions in the book about how to use leftovers, what you can freeze, and what substitutes you can use if you don't have exactly the right ingredients.

For your notes...

For your notes...

The Confident Cupboard

STORE CUPBOARD INGREDIENTS

I have tried to avoid including any hard to get hold of ingredients in this book, so you should be able to find everything in the list below in your local shops (even if they are ingredients you have never thought about before). You don't need to go out and buy it all straight away, build up your collection as you go. This list doesn't include every ingredient in the book, so as mentioned before, read the entire recipe before you embark on your cooking.

- Salt (for some recipes you need coarse salt, for others fine salt is better)
- Black pepper
- Marigold bouillon or stock cubes
- Olive oil (extra virgin for salads, ordinary for general cooking)
- Sunflower or vegetable oil
- Red wine vinegar
- Balsamic vinegar
- Dijon mustard
- Spaghetti and/or other pasta
- Basmati rice
- Tinned chopped tomatoes
- Tomato purée
- A selection of spices, such as paprika, cumin seeds, ground cumin, ground coriander, cayenne pepper, turmeric, chilli flakes, chilli powder, garam masala, and bay leaves
- Plain flour
- Self-raising flour
- Caster sugar
- Baking powder
- Bicarbonate of soda
- Vanilla extract

EQUIPMENT

Again, you don't need to get these all at once, but here are the basics I think you'll find useful:

- Decent knife or two
- Vegetable peeler
- Grater
- Fish slice
- Spatula
- Whisk
- Measuring spoons
- Wooden spoons (I hide one separately for sweet things, but that's perhaps borderline obsessive)
- Tin opener
- Chopping board or two
- A few saucepans in different sizes (non-stick if possible)
- Frying pan
- Colander
- Sieve
- A couple of ovenproof dishes - the tin ones are good and inexpensive
- A couple of jam jars - useful for mixing salad dressing and other sauces
- Measuring jug
- A couple of mixing bowls in different sizes
- Roasting tin/baking tray

Other equipment you might like to invest in if you decide you like this cooking business:

- Juicer
- Garlic press
- Scales
- 2lb loaf tin
- Two 18cm springform cake tins
- Square cake tin

- Square cake tin
- Muffin tin
- Ramekins for individual puddings (I've saved some up from the occasional, ready-made dessert)
- Handheld blender

OLIVE OIL

For your notes...

For your notes...

Good Mornings

Breakfast isn't usually a big deal in our house. I know they (whoever "they" are) say it's the most important meal of the day. But apart from the occasional, weekend extravaganza, it's a bit of a functional meal at ours - fruit, yoghurt, perhaps a bowl of cereal, or sometimes a couple of slices of toast. I doubt you need recipes for those, so this chapter is mostly about the special occasions.

Recipes

Scrambled Eggs

This takes around 10 minutes.

eggs
salt and pepper
butter

This is possibly my favourite breakfast and it's a quick one. I suggest 1-2 eggs per person and one more yolk to make it extra rich - it depends on what else you are having with the eggs. Ingredients you could add to your eggs at the end if you fancy: smoked salmon or ham torn into small pieces, or finely chopped chives. I also like them chef Kenny Shopsin's way, with some grated Cheddar and a couple of tablespoons of sweetcorn - on the toast of your choice.

Use a fork to beat your eggs together well in a mug or bowl. Season with a little salt and pepper.

Melt a teaspoon or two (depending on how many eggs you are using) of butter in a saucepan big enough to accommodate all your eggs. On a low heat, add the eggs and keep stirring gently until the eggs look slightly underdone and runny, then remove from the heat. Don't worry that they don't look done - they'll keep cooking.

Add any other ingredients at the end.

American Pancakes

This takes less than half an hour.

2 medium or large eggs
150ml milk
50g melted butter
110g plain flour
10g caster sugar
2 pinches of salt
2 tsp baking powder
A little more butter for frying the pancakes

These are easier to make if you have an electric whisk, but a hand whisk or a fork would be fine - it just takes a little bit longer. The egg whites are ready when you can tip the bowl upside down and they don't slide out - test this over a friend or family member's head if you like.

You can serve these with chocolate sauce, maple syrup, lemon & sugar, or fruit salad, to name but a few. The recipe (allegedly) serves four people, but you can easily make half the quantity.

Although however much I make and no matter how many people are having breakfast, it all gets eaten.

Separate the eggs and put the whites in one clean, dry bowl and the yolks in another. You need to do this carefully, so there is no yolk in the egg whites (see page 6 for how to do this). Mix the yolks well with a fork, then gradually add the milk and melted butter.

Sift the flour, sugar, salt, and baking powder into a large bowl.

Add the egg, milk, and butter mixture to the dry ingredients and stir gently until you have a smooth batter.

Whisk the egg whites with a clean, dry whisk until they are stiff - so that the egg stands up in peaks when you lift your whisk. Add the egg whites to the batter and stir in very gently with a large metal spoon.

Heat a frying pan on a medium heat and add a little butter - a pastry brush is handy for getting the butter to the edges of the pan (but not essential, you can just tip the pan to distribute the butter). Use about a tablespoon of batter for each pancake - drop the batter into the pan. When the batter starts bubbling, it's time to turn the pancakes over, using a fish slice or spatula. It should take a couple of minutes for each side.

Don't try to fry too many pancakes at the same time - they'll stick together.

Shakshuka

This takes about an hour and 10 minutes.

4 tbsp olive oil
1 onion, finely chopped
1 red pepper, diced
1 yellow pepper, diced
6 garlic cloves, crushed
2 tsp sweet paprika
½ tsp cumin seeds
½ tsp cayenne pepper
2 tins chopped tomatoes
2 tsp sugar
salt and pepper
1 or two eggs per person
small bunch of flat leaf parsley, roughly chopped

I love a hearty, savoury breakfast at the weekend. The fry up (see next page) is a wondrous thing but sometimes this spicy dish of loveliness is what is required.

There are loads of recipes out there for Shakshuka (originally a Middle Eastern dish, much copied around the world): this is just one way of making it, with thanks to food writer Felicity Cloake for testing the many options so I didn't have to. You can make the sauce in advance if you fancy a lie-in. Serve with crusty bread.

Heat the oil in a large frying pan with a lid over a medium heat.

Add the onion and cook until soft and golden, around 10 minutes.

Add the peppers and fry till soft, another 10 minutes or so.

Add the garlic, paprika, cumin seeds and cayenne pepper, stir well and cook for a couple more minutes.

Pour in the tomatoes, then stir in the sugar and bring to the boil. Turn the heat to low and simmer for 30 minutes.

Season to taste.

Using the back of a spoon, make a small dip in the sauce for each egg. Break the eggs one by one into a cup or small bowl, then pour an egg into each dip. Cover the pan and simmer on a low heat for around 10 minutes until the eggs are just cooked. Sprinkle with parsley and serve.

A Classic Fry Up

Allow 45 minutes to an hour to get this to the table.

3 tbsp vegetable or rapeseed oil
8 sausages or vegetarian sausages, whatever variety takes your fancy
1 tbsp butter
300g mushrooms, sliced or quartered
8 rashers of bacon
2 x 400g tins of baked beans
a generous handful of baby tomatoes
4-8 eggs
a fresh crusty loaf (send someone out to buy this on the day if you can)

Sometimes only the full fry up will do. Apparently it can help with a hangover, but you don't need to have over-indulged the night before to enjoy this. You do need a few pots and pans if you're going to do the works. You'll also need your wits about you as there a bit of a frenzy of activity involved - but you don't have to cook everything, choose the bits you fancy.

This is what I would make for four hungry people. It will probably keep you all going till dinner time. You can scramble the eggs if you prefer (see page 18), but frankly this is not the healthy breakfast/brunch option so you may as well enjoy a fried egg (or two).

There are various ways to cook the sausages. I prefer to do them in the oven - preheat the oven to 180°C/gas 4. Add a tablespoon of oil to a baking tray or roasting tin large enough for all the sausages. Add the sausages and cook them for around 30 minutes. Give them a little shake from time to time, to stop them sticking to the tray. Then get on with everything else.

Melt the butter in a medium saucepan and add the mushrooms - stir them from time to time and keep the heat to medium for about 15 minutes. You can turn the heat up for the last few minutes to reduce any liquid. I sometimes add a crushed garlic clove to the mushrooms, but not everyone wants garlic for breakfast.

You can grill the bacon, turning it a couple of times with tongs or a couple of forks, until it's cooked to your liking (probably about 10 minutes on a medium heat). You could fry the bacon if you prefer - no need to add oil to your frying pan for this.

Heat the baked beans for about five minutes in a saucepan.

I personally prefer my tomatoes raw, but I seem to be a lonely voice on this point - you can fry them in a little vegetable oil. If I'm frying eggs, I just add the tomatoes to that pan for a couple of minutes.

For the fried eggs, add the remaining oil to a frying pan and when it's hot, add the eggs and fry till the whites are done and the yolks still a little runny.

If the bread is fresh, have it as it is, if not, you can toast it. Try to get someone else to do the dishes...

Muffins

These will take you no more than 45 minutes.

260g self-raising flour
200g caster sugar
80ml milk
80g unsalted butter, melted
2 eggs, beaten together in a mug or bowl
1 tsp vanilla extract
200g mixed berries (fresh or frozen)
icing sugar for dusting (optional)

This is from my friend Chris Honor's excellent book Big Flavours from a Small Kitchen (it really is a small kitchen - I spent some time working in his wonderful café, Chris Kitch). He does lots of amazing food, gorgeous salads, and cakes to die for. I love these muffins with berries (you can use fresh or frozen) but you could chop up a couple of apples or pears, or add some chocolate chips if you prefer something a little more decadent. Once you've mastered the basics, you can experiment with the flavours. This should make eight muffins - you will need a muffin tin.

Preheat the oven to 200°C/gas mark 6 and line a muffin tin with paper cases.

Mix the flour and sugar together in a bowl. Add the milk and melted butter and fold together (stir very gently) with a spatula or wooden spoon. You don't need to combine these ingredients completely.

Add the eggs and vanilla and fold a few times more, then add the berries and do a final fold, very gently, to combine the ingredients. It's fine if there are a few lumps of flour - it's important not to over mix your muffins.

Divide the mixture evenly between the muffin cases, filling them up almost to the top.

Bake for around 20 minutes until the muffins are puffed and golden, then remove them from the oven and allow them to cool, on a cooling rack if you have one.

You can give the muffins a light dusting of icing sugar if you like.

Granola

This takes no more than 45 minutes.

500g porridge oats
3 tbsp sunflower seeds
3 tbsp pumpkin seeds
3 tbsp linseeds
100g almonds
100g brazil nuts
100g desiccated coconut
pinch of salt
6 tbsp honey or maple syrup
4 tbsp olive oil
1 tsp ground cinnamon
½ tsp freshly grated nutmeg
100g dried cranberries
100g dried sultanas

I always have a jar of this crunchy granola on the go - a couple of spoons of this with some fruit and yoghurt is a great way to start the day. Some of the ingredients are quite pricey, but if you just have a little a day, it lasts for several weeks.

This is a basic recipe - you can try different nuts, seeds, and dried fruit and you can experiment with the quantities. Or you could keep it simple and just follow this recipe.

Preheat the oven to 140°C/gas mark 1.

Line a couple of baking trays with baking parchment or greaseproof paper.

Mix the porridge oats, seeds, nuts, coconut, and salt together in a large bowl.

Warm the honey or maple syrup, olive oil, cinnamon and nutmeg in a small saucepan.

Pour the liquid over the dry ingredients and mix well.

Divide the mixture between the two baking trays and spread out evenly.

Bake for around 30 minutes, until it's turning a nice golden colour.

Remove from the oven and allow to cool before adding the dried fruits. Give it all a good stir and store in a jar or other airtight storage container.

For your notes...

The Warm Up Act

I think of the recipes in this section as starters or snacks, but some of them would be great as a light lunch - use them as you see fit. There is a tomato bias - we just happen to love tomatoes in our house. We've even tried growing them a few times, with limited success, sadly. The tastiest ones are usually from our weekly local farmers' market - just get the best ones you can. The first couple of recipes will really only take you 5 to 10 minutes to make.

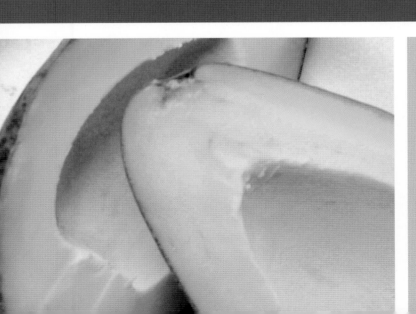

Recipes

Salmon Paté

This takes 5 minutes. Really.

100g pack of hot smoked salmon flakes
180g pack of Philadelphia cheese
1 tbsp hot horseradish sauce
½ tsp lemon juice
salt and pepper

This is ridiculously easy to make and looks very elegant. You can serve it with carrot sticks, cucumber sticks, crackers, or lightly toasted, thinly sliced bread. You can use smoked mackerel instead of salmon if you prefer. This is quick to make and, if you're not careful, even quicker to eat - it's very more-ish. Exercise restraint!

Place the salmon in a small bowl and add the cheese. Mix them together with a fork - it should be quite smooth, with a few chunks of fish.

Add the horseradish, lemon juice, and a little salt and pepper.

Taste a little - you may want to add more horseradish and/or lemon. You can decide how much of a kick you'd like it to have.

Guacamole

This takes 10 minutes.

2 large ripe avocados
1 green chilli, deseeded and finely chopped
2 limes, juiced
2 tbsp coriander, roughly chopped
1 garlic clove, crushed
salt

This is another quick and easy recipe and you can serve it just like the Salmon Paté, with vegetables, crackers, or toast. It's also perfect with the Vegetarian Chilli on page 58 and the Chilli on page 63.

Halve the avocados and remove the stones using a small spoon. Roughly chop the avocados and place in a medium bowl.

Add the chilli, lime juice, coriander, garlic, and a couple of pinches of salt.

Gently mash everything together, keeping some of the avocado pieces whole - you want to see some chunks of avocado.

Tomato and Mozzarella Salad

This is a flexible recipe - you can use whatever size tomatoes you feel like. And you can use more or less mozzarella depending on how much you fancy eating and what size you've bought.

This takes 5-10 minutes to prepare.

For each person:

6 baby tomatoes, one medium tomato, or
   half a large one
mozzarella, a few slices or mini balls
extra virgin olive oil
balsamic vinegar
a small handful of basil leaves, roughly torn
salt and pepper

If you're using baby tomatoes, cut them in half. If you're using bigger tomatoes, slice them thinly.

Slice the mozzarella or cut it into cubes, whichever you prefer.

Place on individual plates or a larger one for sharing. Scatter over the basil leaves.

Season with a little salt and pepper, then drizzle a little olive oil and balsamic vinegar over the salad - use about the same quantity of each but don't drench your salad. You could mix the dressing ingredients in a jar before dressing the salad.

Watermelon and Feta Salad

This takes around 15 minutes.

This is a favourite of mine for the summer - inspired by Yotam Ottolenghi, one of my regular, go-to food writers. He says you MUST eat this on the beach or at least outdoors, on a hot day. But if you live in the UK, that's not often an option. I have eaten this indoors, on a moderately mild day, and it's still delicious!

700g cold watermelon, peeled, sliced, and cut into triangles
200g feta cheese, cubed
a handful of basil leaves
½ small red onion, very thinly sliced
salt and pepper
extra virgin olive oil

Place the watermelon on a large dish and add the feta.

Tear the basil leaves and add to the salad, then add the sliced onion.

Season with a little salt and pepper - go easy on the salt, feta is a salty cheese.

Drizzle a little olive oil over the salad.

Tomato Bruschetta

This takes around 15 minutes.

This is another flexible recipe - again you can use baby tomatoes or bigger ones and you can vary the amounts, this is just a guide. You could use ciabatta instead of baguette. This is a really lovely starter or a snack - we could eat this every day in the summer!

around 6 medium tomatoes or 18 baby
    tomatoes, cut into small dice
½ red onion, finely chopped
small bunch of basil
1 tbsp extra virgin olive oil
salt and pepper
1 baguette
1 small garlic clove

Place the tomatoes and onions in a bowl.

Finely chop the onion and add to the tomatoes.

Tear the basil leaves into small pieces and add to the tomatoes with the olive oil. Season with salt and pepper to taste and mix it all together.

Cut the baguette into diagonal slices, not too thick, not too thin. Toast the slices in a toaster or under the grill. Cut the garlic clove in half and rub into the toasted bread.

Top each slice of toasted bread with a spoonful of the tomato mixture.

Minestrone Soup

This takes 30-45 minutes.

2 tbsp olive oil
2 onions, red or white, peeled and finely chopped
2 medium carrots, peeled and diced
2 celery sticks, topped and tailed (ie chop both ends off) and finely chopped
1 leek, topped and tailed, washed if it looks muddy, and diced
1 garlic clove, peeled and chopped (or crushed)
5 sprigs thyme
2 sprigs rosemary
1 x 400g tin chopped tomatoes
1 litre of vegetable stock (from bouillon or a cube)
1 x 400g tin cannellini beans
200g savoy cabbage (about a quarter of a cabbage)
75g small pasta shapes (such as small macaroni or any other little ones that take your fancy)
salt and pepper
Parmesan cheese

This is a great soup any time of year and has the merit of not needing to be blended, so one less bit of kit required. I like my minestrone served with plenty of grated Parmesan cheese and some crusty bread (which is definitely not necessary).

You can use different vegetables, depending on the season and what you can get hold of. There's quite a lot of prep, but it gets quicker as you get more skilled at chopping vegetables, and anyway, think of how many of your five a day are in this one! It freezes well if you have leftovers.

Keep all the vegetable pieces quite small - and don't worry, once the chopping is done, this soup doesn't take long to make.

Heat the oil in your largest saucepan then add the onions, carrots, celery, leek, and garlic, followed by the thyme and rosemary. Stir well and cook for 15 minutes, making sure your ingredients don't start to go brown.

Add the tomatoes and cook for five minutes. Add the stock. Drain and rinse the beans and add to the soup. Bring your soup to the boil, then simmer for 15 minutes.

Remove the core from the cabbage and cut the leaves into thin slices. Add the cabbage to the soup, then the pasta and simmer for however long your pasta needs to cook for (usually 5-10 minutes). Remove the rosemary and thyme stalks and season the soup with a little salt and pepper to taste.

Sunflower Seed Soda Bread

As a bakery teacher, I felt I had to include a bread recipe. This is one of the easiest breads to bake. You can get up and make it in time for breakfast if you wish. It's also great with soup or cheese.

This takes around 15 minutes.

200g strong white bread flour
50g wholemeal flour
5g salt
7g bicarbonate of soda
55g sunflower seeds
225ml buttermilk

Preheat the oven to 225°C/gas 7.

Place white flour, wholemeal flour, salt, and bicarbonate of soda in a large bowl and mix together with a spoon.

Stir in the seeds and buttermilk.

Gently fold everything together until you can't see any dry flour.

Add a little flour to your worktop and roll the dough in it. Gently form the dough into a round loaf - try not to handle it too much. Flatten the dough slightly with your hand and sprinkle a little flour on top. Cut a deep cross on the top with a knife and place your loaf on a baking tray.

Bake for 20-25 minutes - the loaf should look brown and make a hollow sound if you tap the base.

Place on a cooling rack - this one is best eaten the same day as you bake it, but it does also makes great toast the next day.

For your notes...

For your notes...

Going with the Grain

This chapter starts with a couple of dishes that, rather pleasingly, can be on the table in the time it takes you to cook your pasta. There's a quick and easy salad, followed by a few more pasta dishes. You can use whatever kind of pasta takes your fancy for all these recipes. The chapter concludes with a couple of recipes for rice-based dishes.

If you make too much pasta, when it's cooled down you can put it in a plastic pot, and cover in cold water. Just rinse the pasta and reheat for a couple of minutes in boiling water the next day.

Recipes

Spaghetti with Chilli and Garlic

This takes around 10-12 minutes.

This recipe is really simple and it's all done while your pasta is cooking. When time is not on your side, this is a handy and very delicious meal. If you feel like it, you could have a salad as well. You can't tell in advance with chillies how spicy or otherwise they are going to be. Just saying.

50-75g spaghetti per person
2 to 3 fresh red chillies, deseeded and finely chopped
3 garlic cloves, peeled and finely chopped
5 tbsp extra virgin olive oil
1 tbsp flat leaf parsley

Bring a large saucepan of lightly salted water to the boil. Add the spaghetti and cook according to the instructions on the packet (usually 10-12 minutes).

While the spaghetti is doing its thing, cut each end off the chillies, then cut them in half lengthways. Deseed the chillies by running a teaspoon along each half to remove the seeds and any white pith. Chop them finely - first cut each half into long thin strips and then chop the strips as small as you can.

Heat the oil in a large frying pan or saucepan. Cook the garlic and chillies on a low heat for a few minutes - keep an eye on them constantly, you don't want them to burn.

Drain the spaghetti well and add to the pan, mixing thoroughly to coat with the oil.

Finely chop the parsley and sprinkle over the spaghetti, then season with a little salt and pepper. Really, that's it.

Spaghetti Puttanesca

This takes around 10-12 minutes.

This is another one that takes as long to make as the pasta takes to cook - honestly. You'll get used to how much chilli you like - I prefer this with a bit of a kick. Even if you think you don't like some of the ingredients, add them all - they contribute to the overall flavour. This is excellent with plenty of grated Parmesan.

For those who don't speak Italian, the name charmingly means "whore's spaghetti" - opinion seems to be divided on why.

For 2 people

50-75g spaghetti per person
3 tbsp olive oil
2 garlic cloves, thinly sliced
4 anchovies, from a jar, drained and roughly chopped
a pinch or two of chilli flakes
50g pitted black olives (if you can't get pitted, you have to take the stones out, boring but not difficult), roughly chopped
1 tbsp capers, drained and roughly chopped
100ml tomato passata
2 tbsp tomato purée
1-2 tbsp flat leaf parsley, finely chopped
salt and pepper
Parmesan cheese

Put a large pan of lightly salted water on to boil. When it's bubbling, add the spaghetti, stir, and cook for 8-10 minutes - check the instructions on the packet.

Heat the oil in a frying pan or saucepan over a low heat. Cook the garlic very gently until it's just beginning to colour, around two minutes, then add the anchovies and stir for a minute. Stir in the chilli flakes, then the olives and capers, and turn up the heat slightly until you can hear it all sizzling.

Add the passata and tomato purée and stir well, then simmer gently for about five minutes. Check the seasoning - add a little salt and pepper if you think it needs it.

When the pasta is done, drain it well, divide between bowls, add sauce, and top with the parsley and Parmesan.

Fregola with Salmon

This takes about 20 minutes.

This is a great quick dish and it's really tasty. Fregola is a kind of small pasta from Sardinia - if you can't get hold of this, you could use any little pasta. The measurements here are approximate. You can eat any lefovers cold the next day.

200g fregola
2 tbsp olive oil
1 small leek or 3 spring onions, outer layer removed, washed if they look muddy, drained till dry and finely sliced
100g ready cooked salmon (fillets or flakes)
juice from half a lemon
salt & pepper

Bring a saucepan of lightly salted water to the boil, then add the fregola. Simmer for about 10 minutes (check the packet), then drain thoroughly using a sieve or colander. Leave to cool.

Meanwhile, heat a tablespoon of olive oil in a saucepan or frying pan, add the leek or spring onions and fry till they are soft and starting to brown a little - about five minutes. Leave to cool.

Once the fregola and leeks are cool, mix them in a bowl.

Using a fork, separate the salmon into medium sized pieces and add to the fregola.

Season with salt and pepper, gradually add about a tablespoon each of olive oil and lemon juice - check the taste as you go to get the amount of oil and lemon you like.

Mac 'n' Cheese

This takes around 45 minutes.

50-75g macaroni per person
40g butter
40g plain flour
325ml milk approximately (full fat or semi-skimmed)
about 25g Cheddar cheese or Parmesan
salt and pepper

Perfect winter comfort food. This recipe includes bechamel sauce, which is quite straightforward to make, as long as you don't get distracted and wander off somewhere. It's really useful for lots of different recipes - you'll need it for the lasagne (page 43) or for a pasta bake (cook your pasta, add your chosen filling, such as tuna or cooked chicken, pour over your bechamel, add some grated cheese if you like and bake in the oven for about 20 minutes). You could save a couple of spoons to add to a ham and cheese toastie the following day.

This quantity of bechamel sauce is enough for four people - if you are cooking for one or two, I suggest halve the quantities, but any less would be a bit fiddly to make. Mac'n'cheese is great re-heated the next day and can also be frozen, so I would make at least enough for two anyway.

Preheat the oven to 200°C/gas 6.

Cook the macaroni according to the instructions on the packet. Drain well and return it to the saucepan.

For the bechamel sauce, melt the butter in a small saucepan over a low heat. When it has melted, add the flour and keep stirring with a wooden spoon until you have a smooth mixture. Start adding the milk gradually - take your time and make sure each addition of milk has been incorporated before you add more. You should have a smooth mixture by the time all the milk is added. Add the cheese - you can use more if you'd like a really cheesy taste. Season with salt and pepper.

Stir the sauce into the macaroni to mix it well then transfer it all to an ovenproof dish. Grate a little more cheese over the dish and bake for 15-20 minutes, until it's golden on top.

Alfredo Pasta

This takes around half an hour.

For 2 people

15g butter
1 tbsp olive oil
250ml whipping cream
2 garlic cloves, crushed
salt and pepper
50g Parmesan cheese, finely grated
70g mozzarella, diced into small pieces
50-75g angel hair pasta per person (or whatever pasta you fancy)

This was made famous by The Cheesecake Factory, as featured in TV's "The Big Bang Theory," which we very much love. We actually went to The Cheesecake Factory in Seattle, where they serve this with chicken (as pictured).

If you go for the traditional angel hair pasta, which only takes a couple of minutes to cook, you can do that once the sauce is simmering. If you use, for example, spaghetti, you'll need to check the instructions on the packet and work out when to make a start on that. You can always make the sauce first and keep it warm on a very low heat until your pasta is ready.

If you don't use all the sauce, you can keep it in the fridge for two to three days. Reheat on a low heat in a saucepan.

Melt the butter and olive oil in a saucepan over a low heat.

Add the cream, garlic and a little pepper. Bring to just under a boil. Reduce the heat and simmer, stirring all the time with a wooden spoon for about five minutes.

Add the Parmesan to the cream mixture. Simmer until the sauce is smooth and starting to thicken.

Add the mozzarella to the sauce and stir until the cheese is melted, around five minutes. Keep stirring. Taste the sauce and add a little salt if necessary - possibly not, as Parmesan is a salty cheese. Keep the sauce warm on a low heat until your pasta is ready.

Bring a large saucepan of lightly salted water to a boil, add the pasta and cook according to the instructions on the packet.

Drain the pasta and stir in the sauce.

Spaghetti Bolognese

This takes around an hour and a half, including an hour simmering while you do something else.

tbsp olive oil
onion, finely chopped
garlic clove, peeled and crushed
rashers of smoked back bacon, cut off any rind and cut the bacon into small pieces
00g minced beef (or soya mince/Quorn)
50ml beef stock (fresh or from bouillon or a stock cube)
glass of red wine (optional)
tins chopped tomatoes
tbsp tomato pureé
tbsp balsamic vinegar (optional)
handful of basil
alt and pepper
0-75g spaghetti per person
armesan cheese, grated

I've made a lot of spaghetti Bolognese and lasagne over the years and I think the sauce is pretty damn good the way I do it. But Jessie once asked me to make it "like uncle Patrick does." I decided not to be offended, took it on the chin, and asked my little brother for his recipe. She actually stood over me while I texted him to make sure I didn't simply carry on doing it my way!

You can use soya mince or Quorn (no bacon, obviously) if you are feeding vegetarians or you just fancy a break from meat eating. It might sound like it takes a long time, but an hour of that is the sauce quietly bubbling away, mostly unsupervised by you. This is great with a green salad or some vegetables.

Heat the oil and then gently fry the onions, garlic and bacon till they are soft and starting to get brown, stirring from time to time. This will take around 8-10 minutes.

Add the beef (or soya mince/Quorn) and stir from time to time till it's all brown, around 8-10 minutes.

Stir in the stock and wine, then the chopped tomatoes, tomato pureé and balsamic vinegar.

Leave it all to bubble away on a low heat for at least an hour, but stir every 15 minutes or so to make sure it's not sticking. If it looks a bit too runny, turn the heat up to thicken the sauce.

Tear the basil into small pieces and add to the sauce. Season with salt and pepper to taste.

Serve with spaghetti, cooked according to the instructions on the packet, and plenty of grated Parmesan.

Spaghetti Tetrazzini

This takes around 45 minutes.

This is a Jamie Oliver recipe that I've tweaked a little. It's not cheap, or indeed healthy, as it has lots of double cream and cheese. I've reduced them both by half, but you can increase them again if you prefer.

20g dried porcini mushrooms (or a small handful)
1 tbsp olive oil
4 skinless, boneless chicken thighs, cut into bite sized pieces
salt and pepper
2 garlic cloves, peeled and finely sliced
350g fresh mushrooms, quartered or halved if they are small
200ml white wine
50-75g spaghetti per person
250g double cream
100g Parmesan cheese, grated
a sprig of fresh basil

Preheat the oven to 200°C/gas 6.

Put the dried mushrooms in a bowl and add enough boiling water to cover them. Leave to soak for five minutes.

Heat the oil in a large saucepan. Season the chicken pieces with a little salt and pepper and brown them in the oil, turning them from time to time with tongs or a couple of forks. This will take around 10 minutes.

Strain the dried mushrooms, keeping the water they were soaked in. Add the mushrooms to the pan with the garlic and fresh mushrooms. Add the wine and the strained porcini water and turn the heat down. Simmer gently for about 10 minutes until the chicken pieces are cooked through and the wine has reduced a little.

While the chicken is simmering, you can get on with cooking the spaghetti in a large pan of lightly salted boiling water. When it's ready, drain it well.

Add the cream to the pan of chicken, bring to the boil and turn off the heat. Season with salt and pepper. Add the drained pasta to the chicken and mix well. Add around three quarters of the Parmesan and tear the basil leaves into small pieces, adding to the pan. Stir it all well and then transfer to an ovenproof baking dish. Sprinkle half the remaining cheese on top and bake in the oven until golden brown - around 20 minutes.

Serve with the rest of the grated Parmesan.

Lasagne

This takes a couple of hours, including simmering and cooking times.

1 portion Bolognese sauce (page 41)
6 sheets lasagne
1 portion of bechamel sauce (page 39)

This is my dream winter comfort food. As with spaghetti bolognese, you could use soya mince or Quorn if you want to make a veggie version. Serve with a big green salad or some vegetables.

This uses the sauce from the Spaghetti Bolognese recipe and the bechamel recipe from the Mac 'n' Cheese. I use Parmesan rather than Cheddar for lasagne. This is another one that might sound like it takes a long time to make, but for most of it you're not required to do much.

Follow the recipe for the Bolognese sauce. When that is ready, this is what you do next.

Preheat the oven to 200°C/gas 6.

Place a few spoons of Bolognese sauce in the base of an ovenproof dish and spread out evenly. Place three sheets of lasagne on top. Repeat with another layer of sauce and lasagne, then add the rest of the sauce on top.

Now make your bechamel sauce. Pour the sauce over the lasagne and make sure it covers the top layer of sauce and grate a little more cheese over the top.

Bake for around 30 minutes, until the cheese on top is golden and bubbling.

Risotto

This takes less than 45 minutes.

2 tbsp olive oil
1 onion (red or white), finely chopped
250g or 1 mug arborio or basmati rice
small glass of white wine (optional)
500ml vegetable stock (from bouillon or a cube)
100g frozen peas (a couple of handfuls)
100g sweetcorn, frozen or a small tin (a couple of handfuls)
about 200g cooked chicken or a large tin of tuna
salt and pepper

This is a basic risotto recipe - you can make this with tuna, left over cooked chicken, or indeed buy some ready cooked chicken. I've also made it with fried up diced chorizo and a tin of tomatoes. You can also add different combinations of vegetables - whatever takes your fancy. You need to keep an eye on your risotto throughout the cooking.

Heat the olive oil in a large saucepan over a low heat. Add the onion and stir with a wooden spoon from time to time, until it's soft, about 10 minutes.

Add the rice and stir well.

Add the wine if you are using some and let it bubble away for a couple of minutes until it has more or less disappeared.

Gradually add the stock, a couple of tablespoons at a time. Keep stirring. It should take about half an hour for the rice to be cooked - you'll have to taste it to make sure.

While you're making the risotto, put the frozen vegetables in a small pot or mug and add boiling water to thaw them out.

Towards the end of the cooking time (about 25 minutes), taste a little of the rice to make sure it's cooked. Drain the thawed or tinned vegetables and add them to the risotto, followed by the chicken or tuna. As soon as these are heated through, your risotto is ready.

Kedgeree

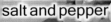
This takes 45 minutes to an hour.

4 eggs
300g smoked haddock fillet, cut into large pieces that will fit in
    your saucepan or frying pan
a little black pepper or 6 peppercorns
1 bay leaf
3 sprigs flat leaf parsley
500ml water
vegetable stock (using a stock cube or bouillon)
25g butter
2 tbsp olive oil
1 leek, topped and tailed, washed if muddy, drained and finely
    sliced
300g arborio rice (or basmati if that's what you have)
½ tsp ground cumin
½ tsp ground coriander
½ tsp turmeric
1 lemon
small glass white wine
a handful of frozen peas
salt and pepper

This is my version, inspired by Nigella Lawson, tried and tested many times over the years and much loved in our house. The origins of the recipe lie in India - by all accounts when we went over and colonised the place in Victorian times, we took a bit of a shine to this dish and brought it back to the UK. But this is a cook book, not a history book, so you'll have to do your own research if you want to know more about that.

The Victorians liked to have it for breakfast and you can certainly do that. We tend to have it for dinner, with the leftovers cold the next day. Great for a lunchbox. You'll need to invest in a few spices for this one, but you'll find plenty of other uses for them. This is delicious with a generous spoonful of mango chutney on the side. You can make your own, but I doubt you will.

First hard boil your eggs by placing them in a pan of cold water, bringing to the boil, and then simmering for 10 minutes. Drain and place in cold water.

While the eggs are cooking, you can start on the fish. Place the haddock pieces in a large saucepan or frying pan. Add the pepper, bay leaf, and one sprig of parsley. Add the water. Bring to the boil, then turn down and simmer for about five minutes to poach the fish. Keep an eye on it - you don't want your fish to fall apart.

Remove the fish from the pan and wrap it in foil. Keep the poaching liquid and strain it through a sieve into a measuring jug (if you have one) or a separate pan. Add boiling water and the stock/bouillon to make this up to one litre.

Heat the butter and oil in a medium/large saucepan over a low heat. Add the leek to the pan and cook it for five minutes, stirring all the time and making sure it doesn't start browning. Add the rice and stir
(continued next page)

Kedgeree (continued)

well. Add the cumin, coriander and turmeric. Use a grater to zest the lemon and add this to the pan. Stir again.

Turn the heat up to medium and add the wine and keep stirring till it has been absorbed.

Gradually add the poaching liquid/stock, a couple of tablespoons at a time. Keep stirring till the liquid is absorbed and then add more. It should take about 20 minutes for the rice to be cooked - taste it after 20 minutes. You may not need all the liquid.

Add the peas, then the haddock which has been flaked into bite sized pieces (not too small or it will disappear).

Cut the lemon in half and add a small squeeze to your kedgeree. Give it a good stir and add a little salt and pepper to taste.

Peel the eggs and cut into quarters. Finely chop the rest of the parsley leaves.

Serve the kedgeree with egg quarters, a sprinkle of chopped parsley and a couple of lemon wedges, if you like.

.

For your notes...

For your notes...

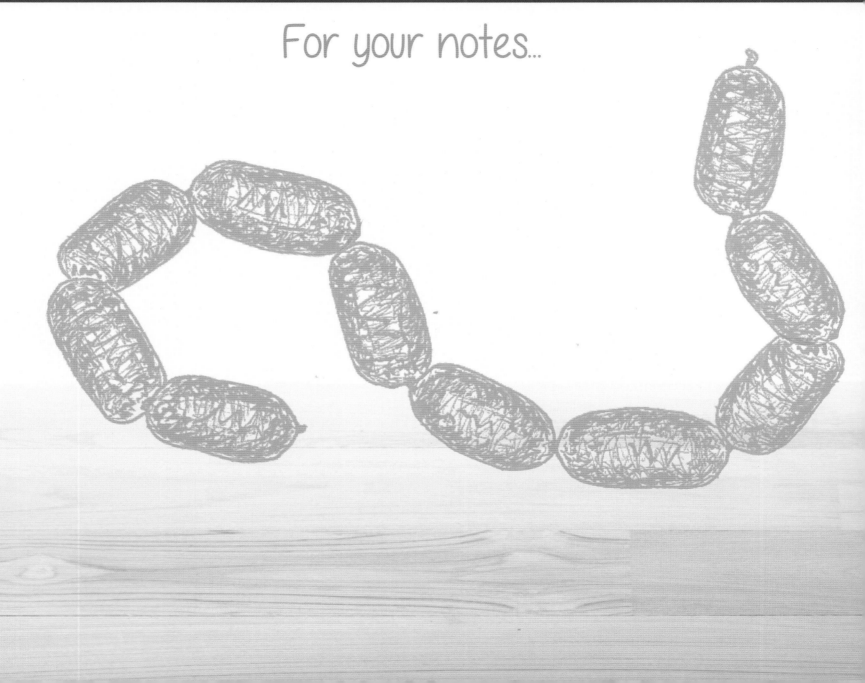

The Main Event

This chapter starts with some quicker and easier recipes and then progresses to somewhat fancier dishes. Nothing too complicated once you've got your confidence up.

It's better for you and the environment not to eat too much meat - you can easily make vegetarian versions of some of these recipes. And you can also check online to find out which fish is most sustainable, as for many of the recipes, you can try different fish.

Recipes

Quick Spicy Fishcakes

This takes an hour and a half, including an hour chilling in the fridge (the fishcakes, not you).

1 stick lemongrass, ends chopped off, outer layer discarded and the inner layers finely chopped
6cm piece of ginger, peeled (scrape the peel off with a teaspoon) and finely chopped
15g fresh coriander, chopped (you can use the leafy end of the stalks as well as the leaves)
400g salmon fillet, skinless
salt and pepper
1 tbsp olive oil

This is one of Jamie Oliver's simple recipes, using no more than five ingredients. We love these fishcakes - so quick, so straightforward, so tasty! These are great with chilli sauce, salad, and maybe some chips. They would probably be delicious in a burger bun too. They freeze well if you have some left over. The cooking time includes an hour for the fishcakes to chill in the fridge.

Mix the lemongrass, ginger, and coriander on a board and chop up a bit more.

Cut the salmon into 1cm chunks. Put half to one side and chop the other half more finely. In a mixing bowl, stir all the salmon together with the lemongrass, ginger, and coriander. Season with salt and pepper.

Shape the mixture into eight round fishcakes (you'll have to get your hands in for this). Put them on a plate or a baking tray and leave them to chill in the fridge for about an hour (more would be fine).

Heat the oil on a medium heat in a frying pan. Fry the fishcakes for a couple of minutes on each side. They should turn golden and the salmon should become pale pink.

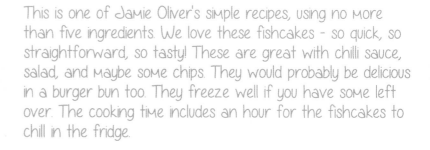

Homemade Burger

This takes no more than half an hour.

A homemade burger is a wonderful thing and so easy to put together. This is a basic recipe - I've assumed you will decide for yourself what accompaniments you want. Personally I like some caramelised onions and plenty of cheese.

500g minced beef
1 onion, finely chopped
salt and pepper
1 tsp dried oregano (optional)
1 tbsp olive oil
burger buns (I like a brioche bun, personally)

Mix the beef, onion, salt and pepper, and oregano (if using) in a large bowl. You can do this with a fork or you can get your hands in there - just make sure you mix your ingredients thoroughly.

Make a tiny burger and fry in a little olive oil for a couple of minutes, turning once. When it's cool enough, taste to make sure you're happy with your seasoning.

Shape the burger mix into patties - it's up to you what size. This recipe makes four large burgers or six smaller ones. Place the burgers on a baking tray or plate and chill them in the fridge till you're ready to cook.

Heat a frying pan and add the oil. Place the burgers in the pan and cook for a couple of minutes, then turn and cook for a couple more minutes. Turn the burgers again, then reduce the heat to medium to cook them through. How long this takes depends on how you like your burgers and what size you've made them - I usually cook them for about 10 minutes. If you want a cheeseburger, add the cheese for the last four minutes or so.

If you have such a thing as a griddle pan, you can also griddle your burgers - brush the griddle with a little oil and cook the same way as above.

Pop your burger and trimmings in a bun and enjoy.

Baked Salmon with Honey and Dill Sauce

This is meant to be served with boiled or steamed baby potatoes, but chips work if you must. The sauce is great with broccoli, green beans, carrots, or any other vegetables that take your fancy.

Takes less than half an hour.

1 tbsp runny honey
1 tbsp Dijon mustard
1 tbsp red wine vinegar
2 tbsp olive oil
1 tbsp dill, finely chopped
4 salmon fillets
1 tbsp olive oil
salt and pepper
1 lemon, cut into quarters

Preheat the oven to 200°C/gas 6.

Mix the honey, mustard, red wine vinegar, two tablespoons of olive oil, and dill until the sauce is smooth, using a whisk or a fork. Season with a little salt and pepper.

Line a baking tray with baking parchment or greaseproof paper. Place the salmon fillets on the paper, season with a little salt and pepper, and drizzle the remaining tablespoon of oil over the salmon. Add the lemon quarters to the tray.

Bake for eight minutes or until the salmon is cooked through (it should have changed from bright pink to a lovely pale shade). Serve with the sauce.

Salmon Chowder

This takes around 45 minutes.

1 tsp butter
1 red onion, finely chopped
2 garlic cloves, finely sliced
2 sticks of celery, finely diced
1 red pepper, finely diced
1 medium potato, peeled and grated
2 corn on the cobs or one large tin of sweetcorn
200g salmon fillet, skinned
150g prawns (optional)
500ml fish or vegetable stock
50ml single or double cream
a small glass of white wine (optional)
salt and pepper
½ cucumber, finely diced

This is another great recipe, ripped out of a newspaper years ago and one that I've made regularly ever since. It's a great hearty main course and it's very flexible - you could leave out the peppers or celery if you want to keep it simple and you could use other fish, such as cod or haddock. It's not necessary, but it's really good with some crusty bread.

Melt the butter in a large saucepan and cook the onion and garlic for around five minutes on a low heat.

Add the celery and cook for two more minutes, then add the pepper, then the potato. Keep stirring.

If you are using fresh corn, carefully cut the corn from the cobs and put the corn to one side. Add the corn cobs to the saucepan with the stock, wine, and cream. Season with salt and pepper and simmer on a low heat for about 10 minutes.

Add the salmon, corn, and prawns (if using). Simmer for about five more minutes to cook the salmon through. Remove the corn cobs.

Put a little cucumber in the bottom of each person's bowl, then add the chowder.

Baked Chicken with Tomatoes and Olives

This takes an hour.

This is really easy to put together - it only takes a little time to prepare, giving you time to chill while it's in the oven. This dish works well with Pasta and Rice Pilaf (page 75), or Dauphinoise Potatoes (page 78), or just as it is with some salad or vegetables. If you use chicken breasts, it will take a little longer to cook.

8 chicken thighs or 4 chicken breasts
salt and pepper
1 lemon
2 tbsp olive oil
12 pitted black olives, (ie with no stones), halved
12 baby tomatoes, halved, or 2-3 large ones, quartered
6 garlic cloves, peeled and squashed gently using the back of a knife
3 sprigs thyme (rosemary also works)

Preheat the oven to 180°C/gas 4.

Place the chicken pieces in a roasting tin and season with a little salt and pepper.

Squeeze the lemon juice into a bowl and add the olive oil, olives, tomatoes, and garlic.

Season the sauce with a little more salt and pepper, then pour it over the chicken. Lay the thyme (or rosemary sprigs) on top.

Bake for 40-45 minutes. There should be plenty of juice from the tomatoes and the chicken's juices should be clear (and definitely not pink) when you pierce the flesh with a skewer or sharp knife.

Ginger Stir Fry

This takes around 35 minutes.

I usually make this with chicken, but you could also use prawns or tofu. You could also just do it with lots of vegetables and it would still be delicious. It's a good idea to prepare the chicken, if that's what you're using, all your vegetables, and the sauce before you get cooking. Once you make a start, it all happens pretty quickly. You can serve this with noodles or rice, cooked according to the instructions on the packet. It's great on its own too.

Serves 2

2 chicken breasts, cut into bite-sized pieces, or prawns, or tofu
salt and pepper
½ a head of broccoli, cut into bite-sized pieces
100g baby corn, cut in half
1 small carrot, peeled and cut into thin matchsticks
4cm piece of ginger, peeled and cut into thin matchsticks
½ red pepper, deseeded and sliced
2 baby pak choi, quartered or cut into thin strips, as you prefer
2 spring onions, cut into 4cm pieces
1 tbsp cornflour
2 tbsp soy sauce
1 tbsp mirin
1 tbsp sesame oil
2 garlic cloves, crushed
½ tsp dried chilli flakes (or more if you like it spicy)
1 tbsp vegetable oil
30g blanched almonds

Place the chicken pieces on a chopping board and season with a little salt and pepper.

On a clean board, prepare your vegetables.

Put the cornflour into a small bowl and add 100ml of cold water. Mix well until the cornflour is dissolved, then add the soy sauce, mirin, sesame oil, garlic, and chilli flakes. Mix again.

Heat the vegetable oil in a large wok or frying pan. Add the almonds and fry for one minute until brown. Remove with a slotted or wooden spoon and place on a plate.

Add the chicken pieces to the wok/frying pan and fry them till they are cooked through - around 10 minutes. Pierce the flesh with a skewer or sharp knife, you should not see any pink meat. Remove the chicken to the plate with the almonds.

Add the broccoli, corn, and carrot to the wok/frying pan and cook for around four minutes - the vegetables should be starting to brown a little. Add the ginger and red pepper and fry for two minutes.

Return the almonds and chicken to the wok/frying pan, pour the sauce over everything. Add the pak choi and spring onions. Simmer everything on a low heat for three to four minutes. When the pak choi and spring onions are tender, the sauce has thickened, and the chicken is heated through, your stir fry is ready.

Fish Parcels

Takes around an hour to make.

I usually serve this with some vegetables on the side. It would also be good with rice, naan bread or Pasta and Rice Pilaf (page 69). You can try this with, for example, cod, pollock, or haddock instead of the salmon.

Serves two - just double it all up for four people.

2 tsp butter
1 onion, thinly sliced
3 garlic cloves, finely chopped or crushed
2 tomatoes, roughly chopped
½ tsp sugar
a pinch of salt
1 tsp garam masala
2 bay leaves
½ tsp dried chilli flakes
1 cinnamon stick
220-240g skinless salmon fillets or other fish
2 slices of lime
a handful of flaked almonds
a handful of fresh coriander, roughly chopped
tin foil

Heat the oven to 160°C/gas mark 3.

Melt the butter in a small saucepan and fry the onion very gently on a low heat for five minutes. Add the garlic and continue frying until the onion is soft - around five more minutes.

Add the tomatoes, salt, sugar, garam masala, bay leaves, chilli flakes, and cinnamon stick. Cook on a very low heat for five more minutes.

Place a large piece of foil on a baking tray or roasting tin. Cut the salmon into large chunks and put the pieces on the foil.

Spoon the tomato mixture over the salmon. Place the lime slices and flaked almonds on top, then wrap the foil like a loose parcel around it all, making sure there are no gaps.

Bake for 25 minutes, then carefully open up the foil parcel and bake for 10 more minutes. Serve with chopped coriander sprinkled over the top.

Fish or Chicken Goujons

This will take you less than half an hour, a little longer if you are baking your goujons.

3 tbsp plain flour
salt and pepper
2 eggs
6 tbsp Panko breadcrumbs (most supermarkets sell these)
400g skinned white fish, such as haddock or cod, or 4 chicken
   breast fillets
1 tbsp vegetable oil

These goujons are delicious with fish or chicken. Either way, they are a big favourite round our way, great with chips, salad, vegetables, whatever you fancy really. The chicken version is fabulous with the Caesar salad recipe on page 72. We usually fry them, which is rather unhealthy but very tasty. I've also included instructions for the healthier baking option.

Place the flour on a small plate and season with a little salt and pepper, mix a little with a spoon.

Crack the eggs into a small bowl and lightly beat with a fork.

Place the breadcrumbs on a larger plate.

Cut the fish or chicken into fish finger-sized strips.

One by one, dip the goujons into the flour, then the egg, then the breadcrumbs. Place to one side of your breadcrumb plate or a chopping board until you're ready to cook them.

Heat the oil and butter in a frying pan until they start to sizzle. Add your goujons and fry for three to four minutes for fish, six to eight minutes for chicken, turning them a couple of times. Drain the goujons on kitchen paper before you serve, to soak up some of the butter/oil.

If you are going down the baking route, preheat the oven to 200°C/gas mark 5. Bake for 15 minutes for fish, 30 minutes for chicken, turning the goujons once, halfway through the cooking time.

It's really important to make sure the chicken is cooked through - I always cut one goujon in half to make sure there's no pinkness to the meat. This is less important for fish.

Vegetarian Chilli

This will take around an hour.

2 tbsp olive oil or vegetable oil
1 onion, finely chopped
2 courgettes, diced
2 red peppers, deseeded and diced
1 carrot, peeled and diced
1 celery stick, diced
1 garlic clove, crushed
1 red chilli, deseeded and finely chopped
½ tsp ground coriander
½ tsp ground cumin
1 x 400g tin chopped tomatoes
1 tbsp tomato purée
1 x 400g tin black beans, black eye beans or kidney beans,
  rinsed and drained
1 small tin sweetcorn
salt and pepper
1 tbsp lime juice
a handful of fresh coriander, chopped

There's quite a lot of chopping involved, but once you've done that there's not much more to do and it's well worth it. No need to chop finely for this recipe - I like to see the different vegetables I'm eating, if only to feel a little virtuous. You can serve this chilli on its own, or with Guacamole (see page 27), chopped avocado, sour cream, grated cheddar, tortilla chips, rice, crusty bread - or any or all of the above.

Heat the oil in a large saucepan. Add the prepared onion, courgette, pepper, carrot, and celery and cook on a low heat for around 10 minutes, stirring from time to time, until they are starting to soften.

Stir in the garlic, chilli, coriander, and cumin and cook for three more minutes. (See Tips and Techniques, page 6, for how to prepare the chilli.)

Stir in the tomatoes, tomato purée, beans, sweetcorn, salt, and pepper.

Simmer on a low heat for 20-25 minutes.

When you are ready to serve this, add the lime juice and coriander and whatever trimmings you have chosen.

Cauliflower and Lentil Daal

This will take around 45 minutes.

There are many ingredients you can use for a curry - this is a recipe I have been using for a long time and I love it. You can try the basic sauce with different vegetables. This is great with naan or rice and it works as a main course or as a side dish with other curries.

2 tbsp vegetable oil
1 onion, chopped
1 garlic clove, chopped
2.5cm ginger, peeled (using a teaspoon), then grated or very finely chopped
1 tsp ground coriander
1 tsp ground cumin
½ tsp turmeric
75g red lentils
300 ml vegetable stock (from bouillon or a stock cube)
2 tbsp vegetable oil
2 tbsp hot curry paste
1 cauliflower, leaves and stem removed, the rest cut into florets (the bits that look a bit like brains…)
300ml coconut milk
125g frozen peas
2 tbsp fresh coriander, chopped
1 tbsp lemon juice

Heat two tablespoons of oil in a saucepan and add the onion, garlic, ginger, coriander, cumin, and turmeric and fry gently for five minutes.

Add the lentils, stir well, and pour in the stock. Bring to the boil, then cover and simmer for 10 minutes.

Heat the remaining two tablespoons of oil in a frying pan, add the curry paste and fry gently for three minutes. Add the cauliflower and fry for another three minutes.

Add the coconut milk and cauliflower to the lentils and bring back to the boil. Cover and simmer for 10 minutes.

Stir in the peas, coriander, and lemon juice. Heat for around five more minutes.

Meatballs with Tomato Sauce

There are lots of different ways of making meatballs and indeed tomato sauce - this recipe keeps it simple. These are delicious with spaghetti or with the Pasta and Rice Pilaf on page 75. You can adapt this basic tomato sauce and add other ingredients if you like.

This takes about an hour.

Tomato sauce:
2 tbsp olive oil
3 garlic cloves, finely chopped
2 tins of chopped tomatoes
salt and pepper
basil leaves, torn

Meatballs:
500g minced beef
3 garlic cloves, finely chopped
about 2 tbsp flat leaf parsley, finely chopped
1 large egg, beaten
salt and pepper
2 tbsp plain flour

For the sauce, heat the oil in a saucepan or frying pan large enough to fit the meatballs in. When the oil is hot, add the garlic. Fry very gently for four to five minutes until it's just beginning to colour. Add the tomatoes and salt and pepper. Simmer gently for about 45 minutes, stirring from time to time and making sure the sauce doesn't stick to the pan. Towards the end of the cooking time, add most of the torn basil.

Now you can get on with the meatballs. Combine all meatball ingredients except the flour. You can do this with a fork, but it's actually easier to get your hands in there! Make a tiny meatball and fry in a little oil for a couple of minutes each side. When it's cooled down, taste it to check you are happy with your seasoning and adjust if necessary.

Put the flour on a small flat plate. Shape the mix into small balls, coat in flour, place on a plate or baking tray, and chill them in the fridge until you're ready to cook.

When the sauce has been bubbling away for around 45 minutes, heat a little more olive oil in a frying pan, fry the meatballs, turning from time to time until they are brown all over. Add the meatballs to the sauce and simmer gently for around 20 minutes.

Add the rest of the basil just before serving.

Elizabeth Taylor's Chicken Steamed in Wine

This will take about an hour and a half, including an hour simmering time.

2-3 tbsp plain flour
6-8 chicken pieces, legs, thighs, or breasts
4 tbsp vegetable oil or olive oil
1 small onion, peeled and sliced
1 garlic clove, finely chopped or crushed
2 bay leaves
2 tbsp chopped parsley
¼ tsp salt
black pepper to your taste
350ml white wine (about half a bottle)

This is one of my friend Jenny's film star recipes. The gorgeous Elizabeth Taylor said of this dish, "I know no way better to cook chicken than this, because it is so elegant. It sounds difficult, but actually you will find that it is very easy." Jenny told me that this is what she makes if she has some white wine left over (!) from a party, "It really is easy, it doesn't take long, and it will definitely impress your guests." Once you've assembled everything, you can just chill for a while, perhaps glam up a little, à la Liz Taylor.

Best not to use really cheap wine (apart from anything else, you may wish to partake of a small glass while you cook).

And the final word goes to Elizabeth, "And that's it! It's wonderful over rice, or just by itself. But do have French bread, or something to mop up the wonderful sauce."

Place the flour on a plate and dip each chicken piece in the flour to coat it.

Add the oil to a big frying pan on a medium heat. Add the chicken pieces and brown them in the hot oil, turning them a few times using tongs or a couple of forks.

Transfer the chicken to a casserole dish or saucepan with a lid.

Add the onion, garlic, bay leaves, parsley, salt, and pepper to the chicken. Pour the wine over everything.

Put the lid on the casserole dish/saucepan and simmer for about an hour, or until the chicken is tender.

Jenny says this serves 6 to 8 people - if you have some left over you can save it for the next day or freeze it.

Fish Pie

This takes just over an hour.

2 eggs
600g potatoes, such as Maris Piper
30g butter, melted
4 tbsp milk (if you're mashing your potatoes)
55g strong Cheddar, grated
salt and pepper
425ml vegetable or fish stock (fresh or stock cube)
150ml dry white wine
55g butter
55g plain flour
450g cod or haddock fillets, skinned and cubed (keep the pieces quite big, around 6cm)
225g undyed smoked haddock, also skinned and cubed (as above)
100g prawns (small cooked prawns are best for this)
1 bay leaf
2 tbsp sour cream
1 tbsp parsley, finely chopped
salt and pepper

We have a fantastic, local fishmonger, where I picked up a recipe leaflet many years ago that included this brilliant fish pie. Once you've got your confidence up, this shouldn't be too daunting and it is utterly delicious! You can prepare the eggs and the potatoes ahead if you like. If grating the potatoes seems too annoying, you could use mashed potatoes instead, but we love it with the cheesy grated spuds.

Preheat the oven to 220°C/gas 7.

Place the eggs in a saucepan of cold water, bring it to the boil, simmer for 10 minutes. Drain and place in cold water.

Peel the potatoes and cut in half (unless they're really big, in which case cut into three or four pieces). Put them in a saucepan of cold water with a little salt. Bring to the boil, simmer for five minutes, then drain. When they are cool enough to handle, grate the potatoes using a food processor or a grater. Place them in a bowl and stir in the melted butter, most of the grated cheese, and a little salt and pepper. If you prefer mashed potatoes; once you've drained them, mash with a fork or masher, adding the butter, milk, salt and pepper, and cheese.

To prepare the fish sauce, make up your stock according to the instructions if you are using a stock cube or bouillon. Add the wine to the stock. Melt the butter in a medium saucepan, then add the flour, stirring continuously. Gradually add the stock/wine mixture, a spoonful at a time, stirring constantly. Your sauce should be smooth and the consistency of single cream. Once all the liquid is added, stir in the fish, prawns, bay leaf, soured cream, and parsley. Peel and quarter the hard boiled eggs and add them to the fish mixture. Season to taste. Pour into an ovenproof dish.

Place the potatoes on top, sprinkle with the remaining cheese and bake for 30-35 minutes until the potatoes are crispy and golden.

Chilli con Carne

This will take around half an hour to prepare and 3 hours to cook.

1 tbsp olive oil
2 small onions, finely chopped
1 garlic clove, finely chopped or crushed
500g minced beef (or soya mince/Quorn)
2 tins of chopped tomatoes
2 red peppers, deseeded and chopped
1 tsp salt
a little black pepper
2 tsp hot chilli powder (or mild if you want to play it safe)
1 tsp brown sugar
2 tbsp runny honey
50g butter

Another film star recipe from Jenny. This is by actor James Garner, star of many a great film and TV's "The Rockford Files." I first made this for one of my favourite days of the year, International Day of the Cowboy (fourth Saturday in July, in case you need to know) and it's definitely my favourite chilli recipe EVER. You can serve this with rice, jacket potatoes, or a big pile of tortilla chips. It's great with sour cream on the side (that helps if you've slightly overdone the chilli levels). You could use Quorn or soya mince if you want to make a veggie version, although then it would be chilli sin carne (for any Spanish-speaking pedants out there). Once you've done your prep, this bubbles away, minding its own business, for three hours, while you do something else.

Heat the olive oil in a large saucepan and add the onions and garlic and fry on a low heat for about 10 minutes. Add the minced beef (or soya mince/Quorn) and keep stirring until the meat is brown, around another 10 minutes.

Add the tomatoes and peppers and stir again.

Add the salt and pepper, chilli powder, sugar, honey and butter.

Stir it all well and cook on a low heat for three hours (stirring from time to time to make sure it's not sticking). Sounds like a long time, and you could probably cook it for a little less, but this way you get a lovely rich chilli.

Toad in the Hole with Onion Gravy

This takes around an hour.

Toad in the hole:
2 eggs
300ml milk
a pinch of salt
125g plain flour
3 tbsp vegetable oil
6 sausages (or vegetarian sausages)

Onion gravy:
75g butter
2 large onions, peeled and sliced
1 tbsp plain flour
a small glass red wine
250ml vegetable stock (from bouillon or a stock cube)
a dash of Worcestershire sauce (optional)
salt and pepper

It seems there is no conclusive evidence to explain why sausages in batter should be called toad in the hole, but I have found nothing to suggest it was ever made using actual toads (which is good, I really don't like toads). This is a pretty easy recipe, you just need to be careful taking the dish in and out of the oven as it gets really hot. But it's worth it. Serve with lots of vegetables. I love it with the onion gravy (thank you Nigel Slater for this excellent recipe), but it's not essential. You can use vegetarian sausages. You can start on the gravy before the toad in the hole if you prefer a more leisurely approach.

Preheat the oven to 220°C/gas 7.

To make the batter, place the flour in a mixing bowl and add a pinch of salt. In a separate bowl, mix the eggs and milk together with a whisk or a fork. Add the liquid to the flour, mixing with a whisk or fork until your batter is smooth.

For the sausages, put the lard or oil in an ovenproof dish and heat for around 10 minutes until it's smoking hot. Carefully take the dish out of the oven and add the sausages. Place the dish back in the oven and cook until the sausages are browned a little, around 10 minutes. Remove the dish from the oven again and pour the batter over the sausages. Bake for 25-30 minutes until the batter is golden.

Now make your gravy. Melt the butter in a medium saucepan, add the onions, and cook them over a low heat until they are golden and soft, about 10 minutes. Put a lid on the pan and continue cooking the onions till they are brown (but not burnt). You can prepare the onions up to this point in advance (but beware, you might eat them all, they are delicious).

Stir in the flour with a wooden spoon and cook for a few minutes, then gradually pour in the stock and wine and stir well. Season with a little salt and pepper and the Worcestershire sauce if you are using that. Turn the heat down to low and leave for 15 minutes, stirring from time to time.

Tomato Curry

This will take around an hour.

1 tbsp cumin seeds
1 tbsp coriander seeds
10 cardamom pods
½ tbsp fennel seeds
½ tbsp black mustard seeds
6 cloves
2 star anise
2 tbsp sunflower oil or vegetable oil
½ tsp ground turmeric
1 tsp salt
tin of 400ml coconut milk
small handful of curry leaves
2 tsp tamarind paste
16 medium tomatoes, skinned and cores and
  seeds removed (see method in the recipe)
1 tbsp fresh green peppercorns, from
  a jar (optional)
1 tsp sugar (optional)
a few sprigs of fresh coriander, finely chopped

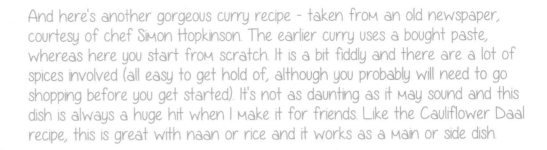

And here's another gorgeous curry recipe - taken from an old newspaper, courtesy of chef Simon Hopkinson. The earlier curry uses a bought paste, whereas here you start from scratch. It is a bit fiddly and there are a lot of spices involved (all easy to get hold of, although you probably will need to go shopping before you get started). It's not as daunting as it may sound and this dish is always a huge hit when I make it for friends. Like the Cauliflower Daal recipe, this is great with naan or rice and it works as a main or side dish.

Lightly toast the cumin seeds, coriander seeds, cardamom pods, fennel seeds, black mustard seeds, cloves, and star anise in a small frying or saucepan for around five minutes. They should start to smell lovely - keep an eye on them though, as you don't want them to burn.

Heat the oil in a frying pan or large saucepan and add the toasted spices. Fry gently for a couple of minutes, still checking they don't burn. Add the turmeric and salt and stir. Add the coconut milk, curry leaves, and tamarind paste. Stir well, bring it all to a simmer and cook gently for 15 minutes.

In the meantime, prepare your tomatoes. With a sharp knife, slice a shallow X into the bottom of each tomato (i.e, not the stalk end), then place them in a large bowl and cover with boiling water. Fish them out with a spoon and place in cold water. Once they have cooled a little, you should be able to peel the skin off easily. To core and deseed the tomatoes, halve them, use your finger or a teaspoon to remove the seeds and cut out any white bits of the core.

The original recipe tells you to use a handheld blender to blitz the spicy coconut milk mixture for a few seconds, pour the sauce through a fine sieve, and pour it back into the pan. If you don't have a blender, mash the spices a little and then sieve - I've tried it and it still tastes great.

Add the tomatoes to the sauce and simmer gently until they have softened a little and the sauce has thickened. This will take 15-20 minutes. Taste the sauce to see if you need to add a little salt or sugar. Add the chopped coriander and serve.

Slow Roast Lamb

This takes half an hour at the beginning of the day and another hour at the end.

2 onions, cut into quarters (no need to peel)
2 whole heads of garlic, also not peeled, cut in
    half horizontally
a bunch of rosemary
1.5kg leg of lamb
1 tbsp olive oil
6 more garlic cloves, peeled and thinly sliced
salt and pepper

This sounds like a big deal but don't worry - it's not difficult. I do love a recipe that tells you to get started and then go off and amuse yourself for eight hours! Once you've got a bit more confident in the kitchen, this is a great recipe for a special Sunday dinner (it's not a cheap and cheerful one though). It's good with Pasta and Rice Pilaf (page 75), Roast Potatoes (page 77), or Dauphinoise Potatoes (page 78) and whatever vegetables or salad you fancy. You may worry that the lamb doesn't seem to be cooking - but fear not, after eight hours, it will be ready.

Preheat the oven to 140°C/gas mark 1.

Place the onion quarters and the halved garlic bulbs in the middle of a roasting tin that the lamb will fit in. Scatter over the sprigs of rosemary, keeping one sprig aside. Place the lamb on top.

Rub half the oil all over the lamb - you're going to have to get your hands involved here.

Using a small, sharp knife, make 12 slits (about 2.5cm deep) randomly in the meat. Push two garlic slices into each slit, then poke a rosemary leaf into each one. Season the lamb all over with salt and pepper and drizzle the rest of the olive oil over the lamb. If you have garlic cloves left over, just chuck them in the tin.

Cover the whole tin with foil and pop it in the oven. Roast for eight hours (read the paper, chill, watch a film or two, tidy your room, whatever). Do check from time to time and if the lamb looks a little dry, splash a small glass of water or white wine into the tin.

About seven hours in, start on whatever vegetables and other accompaniments you have chosen.

After eight hours, remove the lamb from the oven and leave it to rest for 20 minutes. This is the frantic bit where you get everything else finished off.

No need to carve - use two forks to pull the lamb off the bone and eat.

Shepherd's Pie

This takes a couple of hours, including simmering and baking time.

You can use left over lamb or buy lamb mince for this ultimate comfort food dish. You can follow the recipe, but with beef mince - technically speaking you should then call it cottage pie. This is another one where you could substitute Quorn or soya mince for a veggie version. There are lulls in the cooking time, when you can go off and do something else. Serve with lots of vegetables.

2 tbsp olive oil
1 onion, chopped
2 carrots, peeled and diced
2 celery sticks, diced
500g left over roast lamb (chopped into small pieces), fresh minced lamb or minced beef/Quorn/soya mince
1 tbsp plain flour
300ml lamb, beef, or vegetable stock
2 tbsp Worcestershire sauce (optional)
1 tbsp tomato purée
around 900g floury potatoes (King Edwards or Maris Piper are good)
around 50g butter
2-3 tbsp milk

Heat the olive oil in a large saucepan over a medium heat. Fry the onion, carrots and celery for about 10 minutes, stirring from time to time with a wooden spoon until they are soft. If you are using fresh lamb or beef (or Quorn/soya mince), add that now and stir until the meat is browned all over, around five minutes.

Add the flour, then the stock, Worcestershire sauce, and tomato purée. Stir well to mix it all up. If you are using leftover lamb, shred it into small pieces, add, and give it a good stir.

Cover with a lid, turn down the heat, and simmer for around 45 minutes. Remove the lid and simmer uncovered for a further 15 minutes. Leave to cool a little.

Heat the oven to 180°C/gas mark 4.

While the meat is cooking, peel the potatoes and cut them into evenly sized chunks. Add them to a pan of lightly salted water, then bring to the boil. Simmer until tender, around 10 minutes - keep an eye on them, you don't want them going all mushy. Turn off the heat, drain the potatoes really well and return them to the hot pan to dry out a little more. Add the butter and milk and mash well, using a masher if you have one, or a fork. Season with a little salt and pepper to taste.

Spoon the meat into an ovenproof dish, then cover with the mash. Smooth out the top, then use a fork to make lines across the top. Place on a baking tray in case of leakage. Bake for about 30 minutes, until it's all lovely and golden.

For your notes...

The Support Act

You know you need to eat your five a day - here are some tasty ways to do this. Although sadly the delicious potato-based recipes won't help on that front.

Recipes

Green Salad

You can have this ready in under 15 minutes.

1 tsp Dijon mustard
1 tbsp red wine vinegar
around 3 tbsp extra virgin olive oil
salt and pepper

1 large lettuce or two small ones
200g green beans
1 ripe avocado
a handful of frozen peas (no need to cook them)

This is more of a guide than a recipe - it's infinitely variable. You can use different kinds of lettuce, you can add cucumber, spring onions, peppers. Anything green really. You don't even need to stick to green ingredients, although then you can't really call it green salad. I love to add some toasted nuts. The dressing takes a little practice, but it's worth it! You'll have to experiment with the olive oil quantity - you'll get to know what tastes good to you, but the general rule is one part vinegar to three parts oil.

Make your dressing by putting the mustard in a salad bowl and season with a little salt and pepper. Add about a tablespoon of olive oil and mix with a fork. Add the vinegar and keep mixing with the fork. Gradually add more olive oil and keep mixing until you have a smooth dressing - check the flavour by dipping in a lettuce leaf to taste.

Cut or tear the lettuce leaves and wash them. Dry using a clean tea towel or a salad spinner, if you have such a thing. Place in the salad bowl.

Bring a saucepan of water to the boil, add the green beans and cook for three minutes. Drain the beans and place them in a bowl of cold water.

Cut the avocado in half, carefully remove the stone (you can use a small spoon to do this), peel and cut into slices or chunks.

Add the rest of your ingredients to the salad bowl. Toss gently to distribute the dressing.

Waldorf Salad

This takes around 15-20 minutes.

This is lovely on its own or with cooked chicken or turkey. It would be delicious with the Chicken Goujons on page 57. Traditionally this would have walnuts, but I much prefer pecans. You choose. I have to be honest - I rarely measure the herbs for recipes like this.

5 tbsp low fat natural yoghurt
2 tsp runny honey
2 tsp Dijon mustard
1½ tbsp red wine vinegar
salt and pepper
about 2 tbsp finely chopped herbs, such as chives, mint, dill, tarragon, or a mixture
2 apples, halved, cored and thinly sliced
4 celery stalks, finely sliced, diagonally
3 spring onions, finely sliced, diagonally
1 large lettuce or two small ones - gem, cos or romaine work well for this salad
a handful of pecan nuts or walnuts, roughly chopped (optional)

First make your dressing. In a bowl, mix the yoghurt, honey, mustard, vinegar, and most of the chopped herbs. Season with salt and pepper. Taste the dressing by dipping a lettuce leaf in.

Add the apple, celery, and spring onions to the dressing.

Cut or tear the lettuce leaves and wash them. Dry them using a clean tea towel or a salad spinner. Place in a salad bowl and add the apple mixture. Scatter over the remaining herbs and the nuts.

Caesar Salad

This will take no more than 15 minutes.

about 4 slices of (preferably day old) sourdough,
    ciabatta, baguette (in an emergency crouton situation,
    any bread you have will be fine)
2 tbsp extra virgin olive oil (or garlic infused oil if
    you have some and if you love garlic)
2 anchovy fillets from a tin or a jar, drained and
    roughly chopped
1 garlic clove, crushed or finely chopped
2 tbsp mayonnaise
1 tsp lemon juice
15g Parmesan cheese, finely grated
about 2 tbsp cold water
salt and pepper
1 large or 2 small Cos or Romaine lettuce

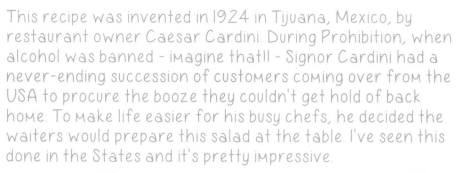

This recipe was invented in 1924 in Tijuana, Mexico, by restaurant owner Caesar Cardini. During Prohibition, when alcohol was banned - imagine that!! - Signor Cardini had a never-ending succession of customers coming over from the USA to procure the booze they couldn't get hold of back home. To make life easier for his busy chefs, he decided the waiters would prepare this salad at the table. I've seen this done in the States and it's pretty impressive.

Caesar would have you make your own mayonnaise, but I'm going to assume you won't be doing that just yet. And if you really want to make life easy, you can buy ready made croutons. You can increase the dressing quantities and keep the leftovers in a jar for a couple of weeks. This could be a side dish or it's great as a main course with some cooked chicken.

Preheat the oven to 200°C/gas 6.

Cut the bread into cubes, about bite-sized, and place them on a baking tray or roasting tin. Toss them in the olive oil and bake for around 10 minutes until they are golden and crispy. Leave to cool.

To make the dressing, put the anchovies in a bowl and crush a little with a fork. Add the garlic and mash them together so they are mixed well. Add the mayonnaise, lemon juice, Parmesan, and water and stir well until you have a dressing that's fairly thick but that you can pour. Season with a little salt and pepper and test by dipping in a lettuce leaf.

Cut or tear the lettuce leaves and wash them. Dry using a clean tea towel or a salad spinner. Place in a salad bowl, add the dressing, and toss. Scatter the croutons on top and the chicken if you are using. You can also grate a little more Parmesan over the salad if you like the idea of that.

Quinoa Salad

This takes around half an hour (less if you go down the couscous route).

This is a great salad for a picnic or lunchbox. It can be adapted to suit your mood - you can change the amounts of the vegetables, you could leave out the halloumi and try it with some left over chicken or salmon. And quinoa is really good for you - high in protein and fibre. Although if you're in a hurry, you could use couscous instead of quinoa - just follow the instructions on the packet.

200g quinoa
½ red onion, finely chopped
¼ cucumber or a baby cucumber, cut into small chunks
small tin of sweetcorn, drained
10 baby tomatoes, halved, or a couple of larger ones, cut into bite-sized pieces
½ tsp Dijon mustard
pinch of sugar
salt and pepper
1 tsp cider vinegar
1 lemon, juiced
1 tbsp extra virgin olive oil
handful dill, finely chopped
1 pack of halloumi cheese, cut into slices or cubes

Follow the instructions on the packet to cook the quinoa. Drain it using a sieve and leave it in a fairly large bowl to cool down.

When the quinoa is cold, add the onion, cucumber, sweetcorn, and tomatoes and give it all a good stir.

In a clean empty jam jar or pot with a lid, add the mustard, sugar, salt and pepper, vinegar, lemon juice, olive oil, and dill. Screw the lid on tightly and give it a vigorous shake.

Stir the dressing gently into the quinoa salad.

Heat a frying pan and add the halloumi. Turn the halloumi a few times, using tongs or a knife and fork, until it's golden all over. Add to the salad.

Salade Niçoise

This takes around half an hour.

2 or 3 eggs
a generous handful of green beans, topped and tailed
1 cos or romaine lettuce or 2 gem lettuces
10-12 ripe tomatoes (you can use baby tomatoes if you prefer)
50g small black olives, pitted
8 anchovies, from a jar or tin, drained (dry them on kitchen paper to soak up some of the oil)
1 fresh tuna steak or a tin/jar of tuna
2 tablespoons red wine vinegar
1 teaspoon Dijon mustard
1 small garlic clove, peeled and crushed
salt and pepper
about 6 tbsp extra virgin olive oil

There are lots of variations in recipes for this salad - this is the way I make it. It's fabulous with fresh tuna, but it's still delicious (and cheaper) with tuna from a tin or a jar. Some recipes don't include tuna at all, but I love it. Some people add boiled baby potatoes, but I prefer this with crusty bread. To have both seems a little excessive.

Put the eggs in a pan of cold water and bring slowly to the boil. Simmer for 10 minutes, then drain and place in cold water.

Cook the green beans in lightly salted, boiling water for about three minutes, drain, and place in cold water.

Wash the lettuce, dry using a clean tea towel or salad spinner, and cut or tear the leaves into large pieces and place in a salad bowl.

Cut the tomatoes into six or eight wedges and leave baby tomatoes whole or cut them in half.

Add the green beans, tomatoes, olives, and anchovies to the salad bowl. Peel the eggs and cut them into 6-8 wedges each. Add these to the salad.

Make the dressing by whisking the vinegar and mustard together with the garlic and a little salt and pepper. Gradually add the oil, still mixing with a whisk or a fork. Taste your dressing by dipping a piece of lettuce until you're happy with the flavour.

If you're using fresh tuna, season it with salt and pepper on both sides. Heat a tablespoon of olive oil in a frying pan. When it's hot, add the tuna and fry for around four minutes on each side - it should still be pink in the middle. Leave the tuna to cool a little then cut into bite sized pieces and add to the salad. If you're using tuna from a tin or a jar, drain it and place chunks of it on the salad.

Add the dressing and toss the salad.

Pasta and Rice Pilaf

This takes just over half an hour.

1 tbsp olive oil
1 tsp butter
8 spring onions, finely sliced
150g orzo pasta
150g basmati rice
450ml vegetable stock/bouillon
1 cinnamon stick
1 bay leaf
salt and pepper

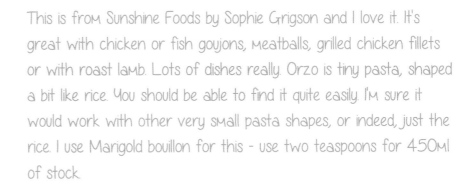

This is from Sunshine Foods by Sophie Grigson and I love it. It's great with chicken or fish goujons, meatballs, grilled chicken fillets or with roast lamb. Lots of dishes really. Orzo is tiny pasta, shaped a bit like rice. You should be able to find it quite easily. I'm sure it would work with other very small pasta shapes, or indeed, just the rice. I use Marigold bouillon for this - use two teaspoons for 450ml of stock.

Preheat the oven to 150°C/gas mark 2.

Heat the oil and butter in a frying pan or saucepan with a lid.

Add the spring onions and fry for one minute, stirring. I suggest you use a timer for these stages, so you don't get distracted. Or maybe that's just me.

Add the orzo and fry for two minutes, still stirring.

Add the rice and fry for two minutes. Keep on stirring.

Add the stock, cinnamon stick, bay leaf, and season with salt and pepper.

Place the lid on the pan and cook on a low heat for 10 minutes. Don't be tempted to take the lid off early. After 10 minutes, all the stock should have been absorbed. If not, remove the lid and let it bubble away for a couple more minutes.

Place the pilaf in an ovenproof dish, covered with a lid or foil, and place in the oven for 20 minutes.

Sweet Potato Wedges

This takes about 45 minutes.

2 sweet potatoes, washed but not peeled
salt and pepper
1 tsp sweet smoked paprika
2 tbsp olive oil

The good news about sweet potatoes, apart from the fact that they are delicious, is that, unlike ordinary spuds, they do count towards your five a day! These are great with a bit of garlicky mayonnaise on the side, in my opinion.

Preheat oven to 200°C/gas 6.

Cut the sweet potatoes in half lengthways, then cut each half into four wedges.

Place the wedges in a large mixing bowl. Sprinkle over a pinch of salt, a little black pepper and the paprika.

Add the olive oil, then mix well to coat the wedges in the oil and seasoning.

Spread the potatoes out on a large baking tray, then bake for 35 to 40 minutes, or until golden and cooked through.

Roast Potatoes

Takes about an hour.

900g large floury potatoes (about five potatoes),
    such as King Edwards
1 tsp salt
1 tbsp goose fat, lard or dripping

I've tried various ways to roast potatoes over the years. This is based on my favourite, the Nigel Slater method - these always seem to turn out lovely and crispy on the outside, soft and fluffy on the inside.

Preheat the oven to 200°C/gas mark 6.

Put the fat in a roasting tin and place in the preheated oven.

Peel the potatoes and cut them into pieces that would take about two or three bites each to eat. Put them in a saucepan of cold water with the salt and bring to the boil. Leave the potatoes to cook for five minutes, then drain them using a sieve or colander. Make sure your saucepan is dry, put the potatoes back in and give the pan a good shake - this helps give the potatoes their lovely, fluffy edge. Take the roasting tin out of the oven and add the potatoes to the heated oil - carefully, as it might spit a little. Tip the pan around a bit to coat the potatoes in the fat.

Roast for around 45 minutes - the potatoes should be golden brown. You can give them a shake a couple of times while they roasting, to make sure they cook evenly.

Dauphinoise Potatoes

This takes just over an hour.

1kg potatoes, such as Maris Piper or King Edwards
1 garlic clove, cut in half
20g butter
about 450ml milk (semi-skimmed or full fat)
about 200ml double cream
salt and pepper

There are lots of recipes out there for this - I don't use as much butter and cream as some suggest, to make it slightly more healthy. This dish is good with roast meat or sausages. It's very popular in our house and I'm afraid to say that I happen to know from personal experience that it's also very good cold the next morning, but that's not what it's meant for.

Preheat the oven to 200°C/gas 6.

Peel and thinly slice the potatoes - easiest way is to cut the potatoes in half, place the flat side down on your chopping board and then slice. (Actually, the easiest way is with a food processor...)

Rub the inside of an ovenproof dish with the garlic. Smear the dish with the butter, using your fingers. It's a messy job, but it's worth it. Arrange the potato slices in the dish, so they overlap. Season each layer of potatoes with a little salt and pepper. Don't fill the dish more than two thirds full.

Pour the milk into the dish until the layers of potato are about half covered, then add a layer of cream until the slices are just covered.

Put the dish in the oven, on a baking tray if you have one (it will catch any drips if your potatoes overflow). After 15 minutes reduce the heat to 180ºC/gas 4 and bake for a further 45 minutes until the milk has been absorbed and the cream has formed a golden crust over the surface.

For your notes...

For your notes...

The Sweet Spot

Eat lots of fresh fruit! But sometimes you'll just want a cake or a dessert, so here are a few of our favourites.

Dessert is mostly a weekend thing at ours, but I do like to bake a cake at the slightest excuse. For some of these recipes, you will need a bit of equipment, but there are also some for which the basic kit will be all you require. Some of them are a little complex, but by the time you've got to this chapter, you should be getting pretty confident in the kitchen.

Recipes

Poached Pears

These take just over half an hour.

300g caster sugar
400ml water
1 vanilla pod or 1 tsp vanilla extract
4 pears

I thought that in the interests of balance, I should include a couple of fruit-based desserts. This is a favourite of mine and really straightforward. You can poach peaches or apricots the same way. These will also be tasty with the granola you'll have made from chapter I for your breakfast.

Place the sugar, water, and vanilla pod in a saucepan (big enough to fit the pears in later). Bring to the boil - all the sugar should dissolve.

Peel the pears (keep the stalks on) and add them to the pan.

On a low heat, simmer the pears gently for 30 minutes, turning them gently from time to time with a spoon to make sure they poach evenly. Leave them to cool in the syrup.

Serve with ice cream (chocolate or vanilla work really well with pears) and drizzle a little of the syrup over the top.

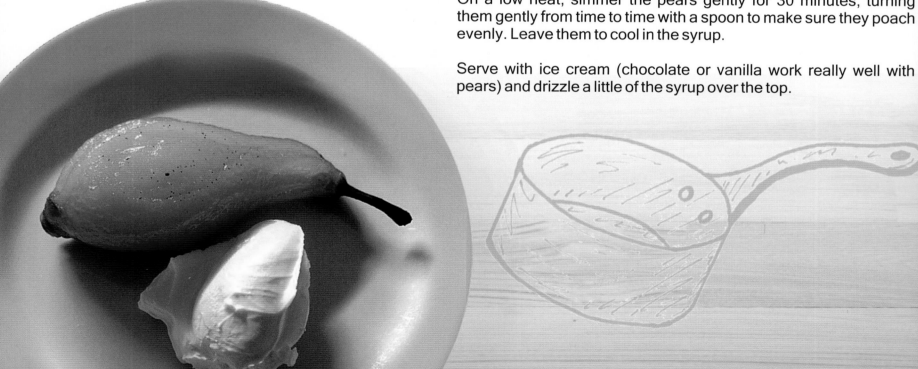

Strawberries in Balsamic Vinegar

Obviously you could just have a bowl of strawberries for a virtuous dessert, but this way is ridiculously easy, very tasty, and rather sophisticated. Once it's prepared, you leave it to infuse for an hour or so.

Takes around 10 minutes to prepare.

00g fresh strawberries, hulled (using a small sharp knife, remove the leafy stem) and halved
tablespoons balsamic vinegar
tablespoons caster sugar
small grinding of black pepper

Place the strawberries in a serving bowl. Drizzle the vinegar over the strawberries and sprinkle with the sugar. Stir gently to combine.

Cover and allow to sit at room temperature for at least an hour.

Just before serving, grind a little pepper over the strawberries.

Apple Crumble

This takes around 45 minutes.

This is quick and easy to put together and it's perfect for a chilly winter day. I love it with apples, but other fruit is available. This is the basic recipe - you can add cinnamon or ginger to the apples and you can sprinkle some porridge oats over the delicious crumble topping before you bake it.

about 900g apples, peeled, cored, and cut into chunks (either cooking or eating apples)
1-2 tbsp caster sugar
150g plain flour
125g chilled, unsalted butter, cut into cubes
35g Demerara sugar
35g caster sugar
a handful of porridge oats or chopped nuts (optional)

Preheat the oven to 200°C/gas 6.

Place the apples in a saucepan with a tablespoon of water and one or two tablespoons of sugar (you'll need less if you are using eating apples). Cook over a low heat for around five minutes until the apples are beginning to soften.

Put the apples in a shallow, ovenproof dish. This is the moment to stir in any spices - maybe ½ tsp of ground cinnamon or ground ginger.

Combine the flour and butter in a food processor or large bowl and pulse briefly, or place in a large bowl and rub with your fingertips, until the mixture resembles very coarse breadcrumbs. Add the sugars and stir well.

Arrange the crumble over the top of the fruit, gently press down, then add oats or nuts if you're including them.

Bake for about 30 minutes, until golden and bubbling, and serve slightly cooled with custard, cream, or ice cream.

Hello Dolly Cookies

These will take around 45 minutes.

115g unsalted butter
85g (6 or 7) digestive or ginger biscuits
70g desiccated coconut
200g chocolate chips or smashed up dark chocolate
125g walnuts or pecans, roughly chopped or broken up with your hands
1 x 397g can condensed milk

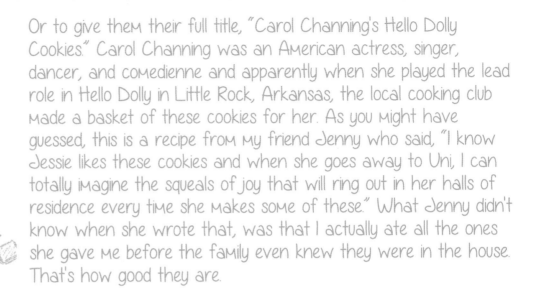

Or to give them their full title, "Carol Channing's Hello Dolly Cookies." Carol Channing was an American actress, singer, dancer, and comedienne and apparently when she played the lead role in Hello Dolly in Little Rock, Arkansas, the local cooking club made a basket of these cookies for her. As you might have guessed, this is a recipe from my friend Jenny who said, "I know Jessie likes these cookies and when she goes away to Uni, I can totally imagine the squeals of joy that will ring out in her halls of residence every time she makes some of these." What Jenny didn't know when she wrote that, was that I actually ate all the ones she gave me before the family even knew they were in the house. That's how good they are.

Preheat the oven to 170°C/gas 4.

Melt the butter on a low heat in a small cake tin on your hob (a square tin works best). Smooth some of the butter up the sides of the tin - this will help you get the cookies out. Remove from the heat.

Crush the biscuits (you can do this by putting them in a small plastic bag and bashing them with a rolling pin or other heavy, but not easily breakable, object if you are not equipped with some kind of electronic grinder). Spread the biscuits over the bottom of your tin - careful, it's probably still hot.

Pour the coconut over the biscuits and spread. Then spread the chocolate chips over the top, followed by the nuts.

Pour the condensed milk over the top of it all and bake for 30 minutes. Let the cookies cool completely before cutting. You can cut the cookies in the tin or take them out and put them on a chopping board to cut them (do this if you're using a good quality tin that you don't want to scratch).

Banana Cake

This takes an hour and 15 minutes.

150g caster sugar
50g unsalted butter, at room temperature
1 egg
2-3 ripe bananas
225g self raising flour
1 tsp baking powder
2 tsp milk
handful of chopped chocolate (optional)

Even if you don't love bananas (I don't), this is a really good recipe. It's definitely tastier with the chocolate in my opinion. You could make this in two smaller tins. Use a blender or food processor if you have one. Most of the time this is baking in the oven and you can be off doing something else.

Preheat oven to 190°C/gas 5.

Grease a 2lb loaf tin (approximately 23 x 13 x 7cm) with a little butter (a butter wrapper is the easiest way to do this). Line your tin with baking parchment.

Place the sugar and butter in a bowl and beat (ie stir vigorously) with a wooden spoon (or a food processor) until your mixture is light and fluffy - as long as your butter is soft when you start, you can do this by hand without too much trouble.

Add the egg and mix again.

Mash the bananas and stir them into the mixture.

Sift the flour and baking powder into the bowl and stir gently into the mixture, then add the milk and mix well.

Add the chopped chocolate.

Pour into the loaf tin and bake for an hour (a little less if you are using smaller tins).

Chocolate Chip Cookie Dough Pots

Takes 30-45 minutes.

150g plain flour
½ tsp fine salt
½ tsp bicarbonate of soda
110g soft unsalted butter, at room
   temperature
85g soft light brown sugar
1 tsp vanilla extract
1 large egg
170g chocolate chips (milk or dark or
   a mixture) or a bar of chocolate

This is from one of the many Nigella Lawson books I have gradually "borrowed" them from my mother over the years - so many lovely recipes.

These cookie dough pots keep well in the freezer in the unlikely event you don't get through them all in one sitting. You can use different sugar if you don't have soft light brown sugar. I've done these with a mixture of dark brown and caster sugar. I have to be honest - this does take a while by hand. If you're doing this, make sure your butter is out of the fridge at least two hours before you get started.

Makes six - you'll need six ramekins or small oven proof dishes. I guess you could make one larger version and bake for a little longer.

Preheat the oven to 180°C/gas 4.

Measure the flour, salt, and bicarbonate of soda into a bowl and mix with a fork or spoon.

With an electric mixer or by hand, beat the butter and sugar in a separate bowl until you have a light and fluffy mixture. Then add the vanilla extract and the egg, beating again to mix well.

Gently fold in the flour mixture, then fold in the chocolate chips.

Divide the cookie dough between the ramekins and use the back of a teaspoon to spread the mixture and smooth the tops.

Place the ramekins on a baking sheet and bake for 13-15 minutes.

Leave to cool for about five minutes before tucking in.

Lemon Drizzle Cake

This takes around an hour.

This recipe is by our lovely chef friend Roger Pizey, who cooks the most wonderful food and has written fabulous books about baking. I defy you to eat just one slice of this cake.

For the cake:

3 eggs
225g caster sugar
a pinch of salt
180 plain flour, sifted
1 tsp baking powder
75g butter, melted
100ml double cream
finely grated zest of 3 lemons

For the lemon drizzle:

100ml water
75g caster sugar
2 lemons, juiced

Preheat the oven to 160°C/gas 3.

Grease and line a 2lb loaf tin (approximately 23 x 13 x 7cm).

Using a whisk and a bowl (or an electric mixer if you have one) beat the eggs until they are fluffy, then slowly and gently stir in the sugar, salt, flour, and baking powder. Add the melted butter, then the cream and lemon zest.

Pour into the prepared tin and bake for around 45 minutes. It's ready when a skewer or cake tester comes out clean with no bits of unbaked cake clinging to it.

While the cake is baking, make the lemon drizzle by boiling the water, sugar and lemon juice together for 10 minutes, then remove from the heat and set aside.

Remove the cake from the oven and immediately brush plenty of the drizzle on the cake. If you don't have a pastry brush, use a spoon to distribute the drizzle over the cake.

Leave the cake to cool in the tin for 15 minutes, then turn onto a wire rack to cool completely. If you don't have a wire rack, you can use one of the shelves from your oven, but take it out before you start baking.

Meringues

These take around 15 minutes to put together, followed by an hour and a half in the oven.

4 egg whites
225g caster sugar
1 tbsp cocoa powder (optional)

This is a great way to use up egg whites, if you've used the yolks for something. You can freeze egg whites and you can also freeze the meringues once they've cooled down. If you just want to make meringues, you can freeze the egg yolks and add them to your other eggs to make really lovely, rich scrambled eggs. So many options.

Preheat the oven to 130°C/gas mark ½.

Line two large baking trays with greaseproof paper or baking parchment.

Whisk the egg whites in a clean, dry bowl with a clean, dry whisk (this is vital - if the bowl or whisk are wet, the eggs won't whisk up properly) until you have soft peaks. As long as you have some energy and stamina, you can do this with a hand whisk, although an electric one will be easier.

Add the sugar a spoon at a time, whisking each time until you have stiff peaks.

Use half the mixture to make plain meringues, shaping into circles with two dessert spoons.

Stir the cocoa powder into the remaining meringue mixture if you wish, then shape into more meringues.

Bake the meringues for one and a half hours. Turn off the heat and leave the meringues in the oven until they're completely cold. You can leave them in the oven overnight.

Scones

These take around an hour.

75g salted butter
300g plain flour
75g caster sugar
20g baking powder
95g double cream
95g milk
1 egg, beaten with a pinch of salt
   for an egg wash

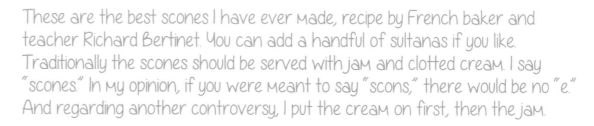

These are the best scones I have ever made, recipe by French baker and teacher Richard Bertinet. You can add a handful of sultanas if you like. Traditionally the scones should be served with jam and clotted cream. I say "scones." In my opinion, if you were meant to say "scons," there would be no "e." And regarding another controversy, I put the cream on first, then the jam.

Preheat oven to 220°C/gas 7.

Rub the butter into the flour (using your fingertips, rub the flour and butter together gently until the mixture resembles breadcrumbs).

Add sugar and baking powder and mix. Add the sultanas now if you are using them.

Add cream and milk and mix until all ingredients are bound together.

Sprinkle a little flour on your work surface and tip the dough out onto it. Press the dough down, fold it in half, press down again, fold again and repeat until you have a rough square.

Sprinkle a little flour over the top and bottom of the dough, cover with a clean tea towel and leave it to rest in a cool place for 15 minutes. I usually just leave it on the work surface.

Sprinkle a little more flour on your work surface then roll out the dough to about 3cm thick. Brush off any excess flour. With a sharp knife, cut the scones into squares (approximately 5cm x 5cm).

Put the scones on baking tray. Don't put them too close together, as they will spread out a little as they bake.

Using a pastry brush if you have one, gently brush the scones with egg wash. You can use the back of a teaspoon if you don't have a brush. Wait for two minutes, then repeat.

Turn the oven down to 200°C/gas 6 and bake the scones for around 20 minutes, until they are well risen and golden brown.

Indulgence Brownies

These take around 45 minutes.

These are very rich and shockingly delicious. The original recipe is actually called "Slutty Brownies," but that's not very polite, so we've renamed them.

Cookie layer:

185g butter
100g caster sugar
85g soft light brown sugar
1tsp vanilla extract
225g self raising flour
pinch of salt
75g chocolate chips (you can buy chips or just chop up a
   bar of chocolate)

Oreo layer:

1 pack of Oreos

Brownie layer:

100g butter
75g self raising flour
½ tsp salt
225g granulated sugar
2 eggs
100g dark chocolate
½ tsp baking powder
1 tbsp water

Preheat the oven to 180°C/gas 4.

Grease a square tin (around 20cm x 20cm) with a little butter. Line tin with baking parchment.

For the cookie layer, melt the butter and mix with the sugars, vanilla extract, flour, and salt. Add the chocolate chips. Press the mixture into the base of your prepared tin, using the back of a spoon.

Next, simply put a layer of Oreos on top of the cookie mix… I like to crush them a little, but you don't have to.

For the brownie layer, melt the butter and mix with the flour, salt, and sugar. Add the eggs. Melt the dark chocolate (you can do this in a microwave, but if you don't have one, break the chocolate into chunks and place in a heatproof bowl. Sit the bowl over a pan of just simmering water and allow the chocolate to melt slowly, stirring occasionally). Add the chocolate to your brownie mixture, followed by the baking powder and water. Spread the brownie mixture on top of the Oreo layer.

Bake for 22 minutes - this sounds very precise, but it seems to work.

Cool and cut into squares.

Devil's Food Cake with Maltesers (or not)

This takes an hour to bake and another hour to cool and ice.

Cake:

225g unsalted butter
225ml brewed coffee (about a mug),
    (instant, cafetière, or bought from a café)
55g cocoa powder
115g dark chocolate (70% cocoa solids or
    stronger), finely chopped
300g soft light brown sugar
2 tsp vanilla extract
½ tsp fine salt
4 eggs
2 egg yolks (save the whites for
meringues)
170g plain flour, sieved
2 tsp bicarbonate of soda

This is a fantastic cake for a birthday or just when you fancy a gorgeous chocolate cake. We love this with Nigella Lawson's Malteser-style icing and plenty of Maltesers on top to decorate. You can go for something classier if you prefer. This icing is flavoured with Horlicks, a malted milk drink, in powder form, which according to their website "is packed with 14 essential vitamins and minerals; it's a tasty treat that also aids in overall nourishment". There you go.

This is easy to make without any fancy kit - although you will need cake tins for baking. It's hard to say how many it serves - it's so very tasty.

Icing:

250g icing sugar
1 tsp cocoa
45g Horlicks
125g unsalted butter, at room temperature
2 tbsp boiling water
Maltesers, as many as you fancy for decorating your cake

Preheat the oven to 170°C/gas 3.

Grease two 18cm springform cake tins with butter and line the bases with baking parchment.

Place the butter and coffee in a saucepan on a low heat.

Once the butter is melted, transfer the mixture to a large mixing bowl and use a wooden or metal spoon to stir in the cocoa and

(continued)

Devil's Food Cake with Maltesers (or not) (continued)

chocolate, followed by the brown sugar, vanilla extract and salt. Stir well then add the eggs and egg yolks, stirring again. Finally fold in the sieved flour and the bicarbonate of soda. Whisk it all thoroughly to combine your mixture.

Divide the mixture evenly between the two tins - you can do this by weighing the mixture or by estimating (I usually estimate, but that doesn't always result in two identical layers). Bake for 30 minutes - the cakes should have risen and spring back when you gently press the surface. Let the cakes cool on a cooling rack for an hour then turn them out of the tins - run a knife gently around the edge of the cakes to loosen them a little from the tins.

To make the icing, use a food processor/mixer if you have one, no worries if not, just use a fork or whisk. Sieve the icing sugar, cocoa and Horlicks in a bowl or mixer. Add the butter and mix thoroughly. Add the boiling water and mix again until you have a smooth buttercream.

Place one of your cakes on a plate, spread half of your icing over the top, add the other cake and cover with the remaining icing. Decorate with the Maltesers (or the ones you haven't already casually eaten).

Victoria Sandwich

This takes about 45 minutes (more if you are going down the wooden spoon route).

around 225g unsalted butter at room
  temperature
around 225g caster sugar
4 large free-range eggs
½ tsp vanilla extract
around 225g self-raising flour, sifted
1 tbsp milk
strawberry or raspberry jam
icing sugar

This is a classic cake - it's a lot easier if you have access to a food mixer, but I do remember "helping" my grandmas make this with just a bowl and a wooden spoon, back in the day. The butter needs to be really soft if you are going to embark on this by hand (but don't be tempted to use the spreadable stuff - it won't end well).

For this recipe, you should weigh your eggs with the shell on and then use the same weight of butter, sugar and flour. It sounds odd, but it works.

Preheat the oven to 180°C/gas 4.

Grease 2 x 18cm springform cake tins with butter and line the bases with baking parchment.

Put the soft butter into a mixer and beat for a minute until smooth and creamy. If you don't have a mixer, use the aforementioned wooden spoon and take your time...

Gradually beat in the sugar, then keep on beating for 3-4 minutes or until the mixture turns almost white and becomes fluffy.

Break the eggs into a small bowl, add the vanilla extract and beat lightly with a fork. Slowly add to the creamed mixture, a tablespoon at a time, giving the mixture a good beating after each addition. This should take around five minutes.

Sift the flour again, add to the mixture with the tablespoon of milk. Gently but thoroughly fold the flour into the egg mixture (use a spoon and stir using a figure of eight motion).

(continued)

Victoria Sandwich
(continued)

Spoon the mixture into the two tins - as equally as you can, either by weighing or by guesswork (see the previous cake recipe). Spread the mixture evenly, to the edge of the tins.

Bake for 20 to 25 minutes or until golden brown and springy to the touch. If you have a skewer or cake tester, this should come out clean.

Remove the tins from the oven and leave for a few minutes. Run a knife around the inside of each tin to loosen the sponge, then turn out onto a cooling rack.

When the cakes are cold, place one upside down on a serving plate and spread with jam. Place the other cake on top and dust with icing sugar.

For your notes...

For your notes...